WESTIES
TODAY

DEREK TATTERSALL

RINGPRESS

RINGPRESS

Published by Ringpress Books Ltd,
Spirella House, Bridge Road,
Letchworth, Herts, SG6 4ET

Discounts available for bulk orders
Contact the Special Sales Manager at
the above address. Telephone (0462) 674177

First Published 1992

ISBN 0 948955 813

Printed and bound in Singapore
by Kyodo Printing Co

CONTENTS

ACKNOWLEDGEMENTS

In order to gather information needed to complete a book of this nature, one invariably requires the assistance of others somewhere along the way and from none more than from those people overseas from whom relevant information is sought regarding the progress of our breed in their respective countries. I would therefore like to acknowledge and say a special thank you to the following people who made it all possible.

Maija Makinen/Seija Maki for taking the time and trouble to gather the historical facts of the breed in Finland. Brigitta Hasselgren, who has been actively involved in the breed for many years; Westies in Sweden would not be where they are today without her love and devotion to the breed. Reidunn Aril, Johan Marheim and Borre Anderson: the three musketeers, hard-working enthusiasts who are helping, with others, to build up the Westie Club in Norway.

From America we have Gary Gabriel, Kathleen and Wayne Kompare, Dr James and Elizabeth Boso, Robert and Susan Ernst, and Joanne and Jaimi Glodek – all of whom reacted promptly to my request for photographs and any information they were able to give with respect to the Westie scene in the USA.

To all the friends in the breed who supplied photographs and information – thank you. At this point I would like to pay tribute to all the Westie fraternity in the UK for the tremendous support and good wishes they gave while I was showing "Paddy" – it was magnificent.

Last, but by no means least, to my wife Joan, a very special thank you. Her unstinting support, encouragement and assistance at all times, made it all possible, proving once again the old adage: "Behind every successful man there is a woman."

Chapter One

THE WESTIE
AS A PET

The West Highland White Terrier, or Westie as they are more commonly known, makes an ideal family pet, and for this purpose it is second to none. While small in stature, it more than makes up for it in heart. The Westie has tremendous courage, it is ever faithful, and it is a great lover of human company. This does not mean it should be regarded as a lapdog – far from it! It is important to remember that this is a terrier, and as such, it is always prepared to stand its corner, if needs be. The Westie has an abundance of energy, and it is very strong for its size, yet content with modest exercise. However, should you and your family be people who like to walk, irrespective of the type of terrain, a Westie will more than keep up with you all day. It is also extremely good with children, which is not surprising, since this breed is a great fun-lover. With all these natural attributes in their make-up, the Westie is an ideal companion for any individual, or for the family as a whole.

When a dog is to be taken into a household as a pet, it must be assumed that the new owners have given the matter a lot of thought beforehand. For example: the size of the dog, plus exercise, feeding and grooming requirements all need to be considered. In fact, the Westie has specific breed features, one of which could be a bonus to asthma sufferers, in particular. Unlike most other breeds, Westies do not moult in the normal way – they do not shed their hair – and therefore some asthma

The Westie is faithful and loves human company.

sufferers are able to live with a Westie when they have found it impossible to tolerate other breeds of dog. If you, or a member of your family, suffers from this complaint, it is worth having a word with the people you propose purchasing from, to see if it is possible to spend some time in the company of their dogs. This will establish if there are likely to be any ill effects from contact with the Westie, before making the final decision. Because the Westie does not shed hair, it will require grooming on a regular basis – every day, if at all possible. This prevents the coat becoming tangled and knotted. A good brush-down is all that is required. However, the coat will grow quite thick and long, and it will require regular trimming, commencing at about six months of age. I would suggest that further trims, approximately every ten to twelve weeks, will keep your dog neat and tidy. Again, have a word with the breeder, who should be able to give you some guidance on this matter – they may even be able to do it for you.

When you and your family have decided that the Westie is the breed for you, what

Ch. Olac Moonbeam: The Westie is small in stature, but more than makes up for it in heart.
Pearce.

is the next move? Firstly, try and establish if there are any breeders, especially breeder-exhibitors, in your area. Start by asking around – talk to your friends, work colleagues and neighbours – you will be amazed how many people have a friend who knows someone who owns this marvellous dog which goes to all the big dog shows! Should these avenues draw a blank, you could contact the secretary of one of the breed clubs; they will be able to give you the names of breeders in your area. Even if the breeder you contact does not have puppies available, they will probably be able to put you in touch with somebody reputable who will be able to help. The advantage of going to a recognised breeder-exhibitor is that you should be able to see one or both parents of the litter, which I would recommend every time. l know these people are basically breeding for the show ring, but not all puppies turn out to be good enough for this purpose, and therefore the breeder will sell these puppies on as pets. This will not mean there is anything seriously wrong with the puppy; it is just that exhibitors are looking at the finer points of the puppy for competition purposes, and they have to be very selective. I am sure that a puppy from this source will be of good quality, and will be backed up with a pedigree, which I will gamble is better than yours!

If you are unable to buy a puppy straightaway, please be patient, and be prepared to wait until one is available at a later date. Remember, puppies do not come via a conveyor belt. Bitches come in season only twice a year, and any respectable breeder will only breed from a bitch once a year at the most. Many reputable breeders advertise puppies for sale in the local press, but beware of kennels that always have puppies available. These people do not breed the puppies, they merely purchase whole litters from what we commonly call 'puppy farms' (or 'puppy mills' in America). These places breed from their bitches every season and are very indiscriminate with their breeding – the puppies' pedigrees are not worth the paper they are written on. I speak on this subject from my own bitter experience.

The first Westie I ever bought was from one of these establishments, and everything that could possibly have gone wrong with a Westie, went wrong with her. The only resemblance to the breed was that she was white. She was far too big in body and long in back. She had a fiddle front, she was barrel-ribbed, she had an umbilical hernia, she was long in the foreface – the list goes on and on. At that time, I knew nothing about the breed, so it was like taking a lamb to slaughter: as I walked into that kennel, they must have thought it was pennies from heaven from the moment I opened my mouth. "Have you got any Cairns?" said I. "You know, those small, white dogs?" "Oh, you mean Westies!" came the reply. "Why yes, of course. Come this way, sir. Do you know anything about the breed, sir? Now here is a beauty, a lovely specimen, sir, a real bundle of fluff..." Anyway, you guessed it, I went home with my prized possession: one little bitch puppy. Despite her numerous breed faults, she proved to be quite a character, but I have subsequently heard of many people who were not so lucky. Within days of buying their puppy they have had to take it to the vet, and finished up having to pay lots of money trying to put things right, unfortunately not always successfully.

Six months later my bitch was looking decidedly scruffy, and was badly in need of a trim, so I made enquiries to find out if there was anybody living locally who could do the job for me. Fortunately I was given the name of Frank Jones, a professional handler of dogs at that time. On the prearranged day I took my little world-beater along. As soon as Frank saw her, he told me in no uncertain terms what he thought of her. He suggested that, should there be a time when I wanted a good Westie, to contact him and he would give me the name of a breeder. Approximately four weeks later, my wife and I decided we could cope with another dog, so we did as Frank had suggested. He gave me the telephone number of Mrs Marion Hampson of the Marank kennels. She had nothing available, but her dog had sired a litter, so she passed me on to a Mr Ian Gregg. Yes, Ian had got a male puppy, but he was not prepared to sell it as a pet; it was far too good, and he would only let it go if the person who bought it would show it. Although the furthest thing in my mind was showing, this was enough to persuade me to have a go, even though I had never been to a dog show before.

My first outing was to a Match Meeting, where we won two matches, and I felt the bug had bitten! The second event was a Limit Show; again, we won two classes in the breed, and were placed in the variety classes. Obviously, at the time, I was convinced the dog I had bought was the best thing since sliced bread – he was certain to go to the top. Then, inevitably, I started to learn a little more about the correct construction of the dog, how they should really show, and what was really meant by good movement. Unfortunately, although my dog was a nice example of the breed, he did not really enjoy being shown. He was quite adept at falling asleep on the end of his leash; his head would become so heavy he could hardly hold it up when he was being shown. In fairness, though, he was very patient with me, and he gave me a terrific grounding in my new-found hobby. I must have spent hours practising the art of trimming on him – it's no wonder he got bored! His call name was 'Prince', and he was so particular, I am sure the royal connection went to his head. He really had to fancy a bitch before he would mate her, so consequently there were very few puppies sired by him! Prince had one other peculiarity – he would never eat meat on a Friday; this was always his day of fast. We suspected he was a staunch Catholic, but how on earth he knew when it was Friday, the Lord only knows! I must say, I did learn a lot from exhibiting this first show dog; he started my apprenticeship, and he gave me many happy hours.

This was the true beginning of my show career, and in fact my wife, Joan, and I had bred and made up four Champions (including two of the breed's top winning Westies for the year each was shown) before I bought a bitch from the Arnholm kennel, and I only made this purchase because the bitch was sired by one of my Champion dogs. This was a real landmark for me, so, in a strange sort of way, a puppy-farming kennel started me on my show career and on to winning Best in Show at Crufts some twenty-two years later – although I hasten to add that the puppy farm deserves no credit! Fortunately, by the time the first bitch was at an age when she could have had puppies, we had learned enough to realise how big a mistake it would have been to breed from her. I can only repeat, *please* be patient if you are unable to buy a good dog right away. At least when the right dog becomes available, you will have the peace of mind of knowing that you have purchased a quality animal, which should come complete with Kennel Club registration. This does not mean that all breeders will not sell a quality dog unless it is going to be shown – my experience was purely a one-off.

Once your new puppy arrives home, give it a couple of days to settle down and to get to know its surroundings. When it realises where the food, love, and affection is coming from, a puppy will soon become attached to its new owners. During these first few days, take the puppy along to meet the vet and have a health check. I am sure the breeder will be only too happy to know that you are doing this, and at the same time you can enquire at what age the vet would prefer to give the first inoculation. The most common practice is to start the course at ten or twelve weeks of age, followed by a second injection some two weeks later. One of the questions most frequently asked by first-time owners is how do they house-train a puppy? A puppy or even an adult dog, does its toilet immediately after it has eaten, so it stands to reason this is the time to put the dog outside. Better still, feed the puppy outside, providing it is not too wet or cold for a very young pup. During the night, place a sheet of newspaper near the door, and more often than not, the puppy will use this.

Two or three days after the second inoculation you can start to take your puppy out on its leash to encounter the big wide world. This is also a good time to introduce your pup to travelling in the car. Start by going short distances at first, and then go on longer trips as the dog gets older. If this is done gradually, the dog will have no fear about travelling. On the contrary, my dogs have always been eager to travel with the family, and they do not like being left out of the party. A few words of warning: please do not leave your dog alone in the car with all the windows shut, especially in the warmer weather. Far too many dogs have died of dehydration because of this lack of care by owners who have gone walkabout, for one reason or another. It is all too easy to be out in the fresh air, and fail to realise that the temperature in the car is building up to unbearable degrees, and this can happen within a very short space of time.

If you have not already thought about it, you will soon realise that puppies like to chew, particularly when they start cutting their second teeth, at approximately sixteen weeks of age. One tip is to collect a few empty plastic lemonade bottles, a pair of discarded tights with a knot in them, and an old slipper or shoe. Put these in a special corner of the room where the pup can find them. I have found that this works wonders, and, to date, we have had no chewed furniture. However, should you or one of the family leave your best shoes lying around and these get damaged by chewing, do not blame the dog – it is only one person's fault – and you know who that is as well as I do. It is also worth warning the first-time owner that the Westie is an 'earth dog', and, as such, it is a great digger. It must therefore be taught at a very early age that it must not play havoc with your favourite flower bed! However, do not be too harsh with your puppy, for it is only obeying a natural instinct.

Despite these words of warning, I am sure once you and your dog get to know each other, you will have a great relationship – the Westie is so easy to get along with. The average life-span of the breed is between twelve and fifteen years;

therefore, it is vital to remember that a dog is there for life. So go and enjoy each other's company – I can guarantee that you will find no better canine companion.

Chapter Two

ORIGINS
AND HISTORY

Every Westie enthusiast is interested in the origins of the breed, but as with all breeds it is difficult to trace exactly when the West Highland White Terrier emerged as a distinctive type. They have certainly been family favourites for a long time, and there are a number of old paintings depicting scenes of the Scottish Highlands and including a little white dog. One such painting is titled "Dignity and Impudence" and is by the very famous Victorian artist Sir Edwin Landseer, dated 1839.

Most breeds are the result of cross breeding, and the West Highland is no exception. There have been a number of theories put forward, as to which breeds were used in the make-up of the Westie, but the favourite seems to be a cross between a Scottish Terrier, or Aberdeen Terrier as they were once more commonly known, and the Cairn Terrier. I have seen some old photographs, two of which were American Champions Hookwood Showman and Pamela Of Hillandale, and by today's standards they would be identified as wheaten-coloured Scottish Terriers – even the style of trimming would suggest this. Similarly, there are a lot of dogs of the same era which very much resemble a Cairn. I am not trying to denigrate these dogs, but to show how it is perfectly possible for the Westie to have evolved from a cross of the two breeds. I think it would be fair to say the breed has stabilised in its type since the Second World War. This probably occurred because many people had

A very early type of West Highland White Terrier (approx. 1900).

The Cairn Terrier and the Scottish Terrier both contributed to the make-up of the Westie as a separate breed. (1914)

A very rare photograph showing Colonel Malcolm's original "Poltalloch Eleven".

Early Westies in the show ring (approx. 1925): Chum Of Chadwick (top) and Cooden Sue.

to give up their dogs during the war years due to food shortages. Dog shows, also, had to become a thing of the past; and so, with so few dogs left to breed from, a type was stamped and became established.

The first strains of the West Highland Terrier as a breed are attributed to the Malcolm family from Poltalloch, Argyllshire. In fact, Colonel Malcolm is generally considered to be the founder of the breed. He had a complete kennel of White Terriers, and he is credited with naming the breed West Highland White Terrier. It is believed that this hardy terrier, with its white coat, was basically bred so it could easily be seen from a distance, when it was hunting in the Highlands among the heather and the rocks. Small white terriers were also used on the Duke of Argyll's estate at Roseneath, where they were called Roseneath Terriers. They were generally regarded as being of the same species, and eventually they were grouped under the same banner as Colonel Malcolm's West Highland White Terriers.

Over the years a number of books have been written about the West Highland White Terrier. The majority give a detailed account of the history of the breed and its early years in the show ring. It is therefore my intention to highlight the more recent history of the breed. At the end of the Second World War those breeders who had managed to hang on to a few dogs, banded together to set about reviving the breed. These people were of course the legendary Mrs Pacey of the Wolvey fame, Miss Turnbull (Leal), Miss Write (Calunna), Mr Beels (O'Petriburg), Miss Wade (Freshney) and Dr and Mrs Russell (Crubens). It goes without saying, the breed today owes a great debt of gratitude to these old stalwarts, along with a number of

Ch. Wolvey Poacher, owned by Mrs Pacey. (1934.)

lesser known enthusiasts of the time. On the next occasion you are either trimming, showing, or just walking your dog, it is worth remembering that you would not be able to do this if it had not been for those tenacious guardians of the breed. These are the people who managed to keep the breed alive during those dark days. It is impossible to confirm, but it is thought that there was only one stud dog left after the war, and that was Miss Wade's Hookwood Mentor. I am also informed this dog was a monorchid, and if we are to believe that monorchidism is hereditary, it is more than likely that this problem will appear in the breed. I have always been convinced this condition is on every breeding line, and although it is not a serious problem, it is one that comes to the surface every now and again, and it is interesting to see where it comes from.

When I came into the breed twenty-three years ago, you could still look at the pedigrees of dogs, and see many of the old kennel names. Alongside these were the names of the top offspring of the time, and the names of kennels which were the new backbone of the breed. Unfortunately, because of the passage of time and the passing on of some of these people, we are now beginning to lose these names from the pedigrees. I sometimes think it would be nice if The West Highland White Terrier of England Club, of which I am a proud member, was able to start collecting past and present pedigrees of the top dogs in the breed. These would be the property of the club, and a print-out could be displayed at, say, the Club Championship Shows. As the Westie is a British dog this would be an unparalleled reference for all those involved in the breed, both in the UK and overseas. This is the history of our breed, and I believe we should cherish it.

A number of kennels have had a very significant influence on the breed over the

A series of cigarette cards issued by Players:

1925.

1929.

1938.

1931.

years, and Mrs Pacey with her Wolvey line immediately springs to mind. To most people she was a true doyenne of the breed. The Branston prefix, belonging to Mr and Mrs Dennis also played a very important role. There was a time when I doubt whether you could pick up a pedigree without seeing a Wolvey or Branston dog featured in there somewhere. Rightly or wrongly, I always felt the Wolvey line were particularly strong in bitches – they were always very feminine. The most impressive of the Dennis's dogs was Ch. Barrister of Branston, who made a very big impact on the breed. Another dog which was represented on many pedigrees was Ch. Calluna The Poacher, owned by Mrs Beels and bred by Miss Audrey Write. This dog went on to sire a number of Champions. It is impossible to move on in time without mentioning Mrs Finch and her dog, Ch. Shiningcliff Simon (Ch. Leal Flurry – Walney Thistle). This dog was the first Westie to win Best Terrier at Crufts, in 1950, and I am sure that he helped to create a greater interest in the breed.

There were two notable dogs from Mrs Samson's Quakertown kennel – Ch. Quakertown Quistador and Ch. Quakertown Quandry. Today, there are still one or

Ch. Pillerton Peterman: successful in the show ring in Britain and America.
Owned by Sylvia Kearsey.

two kennels whose kennel roots go back to the Quakertown dogs. Ch. Sollershott
Soloist (Ch. Bandsman Of Branston – Citrus Silhouette) was shown in the ring just
before I came into the breed, but looking at photographs, he always made an
impression with me. He was bred and shown by Mrs Kenney-Taylor. Alas, this lady
retired from breeding and showing before I started my kennel. She was highly
influential during her relatively short time in the breed. Mrs Beer and her Whitebriar
kennel enjoyed considerable success over the years. Ch.Whitebriar Jonfair
(Whitebriar Johncock – Whitebriar Jeenay) was the last of a long list of Champions
from this kennel. I remember this dog well, for he was the dog leading the field
when I started showing my own young dog, Ch. Olac Moonraker (Pillerton Perry –
Miranda Moon Of Olac). As my young fellow started to mature, we would come up
against and be challenging Jonfair on numerous occasions.

Ch. Birkfell Student Prince: gained his title when he was twelve years old. Owned by Mrs Sheila Clelland.

Mrs Sylvia Kearsey with her Pillerton line made a significant contribution to the breed. Without doubt, the most outstanding dog she bred was Ch. Pillerton Peterman (Slitrig Simon – Pillerton Pickle). Not only did he do well in this country, both in the show ring and as a sire, but he also went to America with Sylvia and was highly successful in both fields. Miss Sheila Clelland, of the Birkfell prefix has been a long-standing and active member of the Westie show scene, and has bred a number of Champions in the UK, as well as exporting stock which has done well in the adopted countries. In fact, Sheila holds the record for the oldest dog to become a Champion in the breed: Ch. Birkfell Student Prince gained his title when he was twelve years old.

A history of the West Highland White Terrier would not be complete without reference to Miss F. Cook and her Famecheck lineage. Here again, I very much

Ch. Highstile Prank: a fine representative of Mr and Mrs Wyn Bertram's Highstile kennel.

Ch. Olac Moondream. McFarlane.

Ch. Lasara Leading Lady.   *Dalton.*

doubt if you could pick up one of today's pedigrees without finding a Famecheck dog or bitch somewhere on it. She had many fine dogs, but I must make a special mention of a bitch she showed in the seventies. This was Ch. Famecheck Glamis, a very feminine bitch with plenty of character. She was short in back with tail on top; she showed and moved with style. The Highstile kennel, owned by Mr and Mrs Wyn Bertram always produced dogs of quality. They were never shown a great deal, but when they had a representative you could always guarantee nice stock and hot competition. One of my favourites, which Wyn was particularly proud of, was Ch. Highstile Prank. Sadly we lost Mr Bertram this year, a quiet man with quite a wit, but in every sense a gentleman. The first Westie to achieve the coveted prize of Best in Show at Crufts was Ch. Dianthus Buttons (Alpin Of Kendrum – Starcyl Sioux) in 1976. He was bred by Kathleen Newstead, co-owned by Mrs Dorothy Taylor, and handled by Geoff Corrish. Both Kathleen and Dorothy disappeared from the show scene soon after their big win.

Unfortunately, we now have a situation in Scotland where there are very few breeder-exhibitors any more. Some years ago Mrs Jean Taylor and her daughter

Ch. Lasara Hell Of A Girl.   *Dalton.*

Leslie, of the Checkbar prefix, produced some fine dogs. Their first Champion was Ch. Checkbar Donsie Kythe, who gained his title in 1969. He was followed in the same year by Ch. Checkbar Remony Rye. Two more Champions were to follow: Ch. Checkbar Tommy Quite Right in 1971, and Ch. Checkbar Findlay McDougal in 1974. Sad to say, Jean died, followed very shortly by the death of Leslie at the tender age of twenty-one. Mr and Mrs Berry and their son Douglas, with the Incheril kennel, are actively showing and breeding Westies in Scotland, and so are Alan and Lottie Bonus of the Tasman prefix. The very first dog I used at stud for my first litter was Ch. Tasman March Of Time. It was from this litter that I kept a bitch, Miranda Moon Of Olac, who produced my first Champion, Ch. Olac Moonraker, and my third Champion, Ch. Olac Moondrift. I therefore had a very soft spot for this dog, which went on to produce a number of other Champions. Mrs J. Sinclair, nee Herbert, (Glenalwyne) was very active in the show ring a few years ago, when she extensively campaigned Ch. Glenalwyne Sonny Boy, followed by his litter sister Ch. Glenalwyne Shieldo. Both were handled by the well-known professional handler,

Ch. Jaimont Of Whitebriar: Winner of the Terrier Group at Crufts 1984.   Pearce.

Ch. Pepabby Poacher: Best of Breed at Crufts 1987.

Ch. Brierlow Beezneez.

Ernest Sharp. Sonny Boy went on to be the breed record holder for twelve years with his tally of thirty-three CCs, only to relinquish this record to my own dog, Ch. Olac Moonpilot (Olac Moonmaverick – Olac Wintermoon) who holds the record with forty-eight CCs.

The Lasara kennel of Mrs Barbara Graham has been very active for a number of years, and her first Champion came along in the shape of Ch. Lasara Lee in 1963. In the seventies, Barbara was joined by Jane Kabel from Holland, who brought back with her Int. Dutch Ch. Lasara Lots Of Fun. This dog was bred by Barbara and Mrs Hazell, and very quickly gained his English title. The partnership was very successful until Jane moved back to Holland, where she has continued to successfully breed and show her Westies. In the meantime, the Lasaras are continuing in their winning ways with Ch. Lasara Leading Lady, and Ch. Lasara Hell Of A Girl, the latter being owned by Mrs Dot Britten (Krisma).

A number of other kennels have come to the fore in the last twenty years, including Ron and Betty Armstrong's Justrite kennel. Among the proudest moments in their show career was when they won the Terrier Group at Crufts in 1984 with Ch. Jaimont Of Whitebriar, and later winning Best in Show at the National Terrier in 1986, with Ch. Ballacoar Jinny Is Justrite. This last big win was a particular pleasure to me because I had judged the breed and given her the Best of Breed on the day. Another to have made great strides over the last two decades is Sue Thomson's

Eng. Span. Ch. Ashgate Connel: a son of Eng. Span. Ch. Ashgate Sallachy.
Bred by Sue Thomson.

Ashgate kennel. One very striking bitch is Ch. Ashgate Sallachy (Ch. Ashgate Achnasheen – Ch. Ashgate Skara), with her son Ch. Ashgate Connel (IKC Ch. Ashgate Kirkcowan Of Poolmist – Ch. Ashgate Sallachy) who was bred by Sue. Both of these dogs have since been sold to Spain from where they are continuing their winning ways on the continent. I recently judged the breed in Belgium, and without realising who they were, I gave this pair the Best Dog and Best Bitch, with Sallachy getting the nod and going Best of Breed. Naturally, I was pleased to see

Ch. Kwickstep Of Kristajen: top Westie puppy in 1988 and top Westie bitch in 1990. Bred by Doreen Lancaster, owned and handled by Jean Abbey.

Ch. Ballacoar Miss Muslin Of Clanestar: Best Terrier at the Border Union Show.

Dalton.

Ch. Ballacoar Jinny.

Ch. Cabon Sea Lord: a son of the highly successsful Ch. Domaroy, who has produced Champions in Britain and overseas.

Ch. Olac Moonpilot: Crufts Best in Show 1990 and breed record holder with forty-eight CCs.   *Marc Henrie.*

her go on to win Best Terrier in Show, but imagine my surprise when it was pointed out to me later that I had given Sallachy her first CC when she was shown in England, some time before her departure overseas.

Two ladies, who have successfully joined forces by working very closely together with their showing and breeding programme, are Jean Abbey (Kristajen), and Doreen Lancaster (Clanestar). One of the results of their combined efforts is Ch. Kwickstep Of Kristajen (Ch. Kristajen Charterman – Clanestar Carryon), bred by Doreen but owned and shown by Jean. This bitch was top Westie puppy in the UK in 1988, and top Westie bitch in 1990 with six CCs and six Reserve CCs. Another bitch with a good show career, who is owned and shown by Doreen and bred by Mrs Morgan, is Ch. Ballacoar Miss Muslin Of Clanestar. I gave her the Best of Breed at the Border Union show on a very hot summer's day, and without flagging she went on to win Best Terrier. It always gives me a special thrill when the dog or bitch which I have given Best of Breed to, goes on to win higher honours. This was the case when my Best of Breed, Ch. Haweswalton Houdini, belonging to Sue Hawes, once again went Best Terrier when I judged at Blackpool.

The Domaroy kennel, owned by Dorothy and Roy Wilshaw, has also made its mark on the breed in the recent past. Possibly the best dog of many good animals they have bred to date must be Ch. Domaroy Saracen (Ch. Tasman March of Time – Ch. Domaroy Erisort Serenade). Not only was he successful in the show ring, but he has proved himself to be a fine producer of quality dogs. Many of his offspring have gained their Championship titles in this country, and abroad. It is remarkable that the Ashgate, Domaroy, Justrite, and our own Olac kennel all started at approximately the same time, and our show careers have run fairly parallel all along the way. In 1980 my own young bitch, Ch. Halfmoon Of Olac (Eng. Am. Can. Ch. Olac Moondrift – Temperly Tangerine), bred by Mr and Mrs Parr of the Arnholm kennel, won Top Puppy All Breeds in Britain. This was a competition organised at that time by Spillers Dog Food and *Dog World,* the canine paper. She went on to win sixteen CCs, and to this day she still holds the record for top winning bitch in the breed.

At this point I think I can be excused for extolling the virtues of my own dog, Ch. Olac Moonpilot, or "Paddy" as he is affectionately known, but his show record was quite remarkable. My first show with Paddy was at a Terrier open show when he was ten months old, where he went Best Puppy in Show. The breed judge was Mrs Pat Barrel (Barwest), and the main judge was Ted Hutchinson, who showed Brannigan the Border Terrier to Reserve Best in Show at Crufts in 1988. Paddy's next venture in the ring was at a large all breeds open show, where he not only went Best Puppy in Show, but also took Best in Show. The judge on this occasion was Miss McClaran of the famous Deansgate Miniature Schnauzers. Mrs Jean Wharmby

(Chatterdale) was the next breed specialist to judge Paddy at another Terrier open show, and here he got Best of Breed, Best Puppy in Show, and Reserve Best in Show. He then went on to Manchester, his first Championship show, at the age of thirteen months. On this occasion he was awarded the Reserve CC, under Mrs Hilda Varley (Yelrav), and this was especially pleasing since he had only just started his show career. Paddy was a late developer, and this was the reason for his relatively late arrival in the show ring. He is the perfect example for demonstrating that you should not be in too much of a hurry to enter shows with a puppy. Learn to recognise quality, and wait until the dog is ready.

The Scottish Breeds Championship Show was his next event, and the breed judge was Mrs Barbara Graham (Lasara), who gave him Best of Breed. Against all expectations, the Best in Show judge, Mr Ernest Frogget, the all-rounder, gave Paddy his first top award. These are times you dream about, and I came home on cloud nine! Without going into each show, blow by blow, suffice to say that Paddy eventually amassed a record forty-eight CCs, twelve Reserve CCs, eighteen Terrier Groups, nine Reserve Terrier Groups, ten Best in Shows, and six Reserve Best in Shows – all of these awards being at general Championship shows. In addition, he was Best in Show at Breed Specialty Shows no less than four times. Interestingly, in the first year that Paddy was shown, he got Best of Breed at Leeds Championship Show. The Terrier Group judge on the day was Mrs Ferrelith Sommerfield, who pulled him out in the final, out of five dogs. We did not win on this occasion, but Mrs Summerfield wrote in her critique: "An outstanding young dog, one for the future." How right she was – for it was the same Mrs Sommerfield who gave him Best in Show at Crufts, some two years later.

Chapter Three

THE BREED STANDARD

The Breed Standard is so vital, I do not think we can look at it too often, whether we be breeder, exhibitor or judge. More importantly, we must all learn to interpret it, as it is written. Some people have a nasty habit of trying to convince others that the Standard is whatever they are showing at that time. They are not only endeavouring to fool others but, regrettably and more importantly, they are fooling themselves. This attitude does not do the breed any good, and it just proves that the individual is in the sport of dog showing for the wrong reasons. The Breed Standard, as laid down by the English Kennel Club, and the FCI Standard are very similar, with just a slight difference in the American Kennel Club Standard. I have therefore included all three Standards for comparison. The UK Standard is a fairly recent update, and is more explicit than the previous Standard; it is now laid out to be a little more in keeping with the American Standard. When reading the two Breed Standards I am sure you will agree the American Standard goes into a little more detail on the various points of the breed compared with the British version, and in some ways it is a little more descriptive on each aspect, with more obvious help to the novice. One of the main differences is size. In the UK there are no set differences between dogs and bitches; we categorise all Westies as being approximately eleven inches in height to the

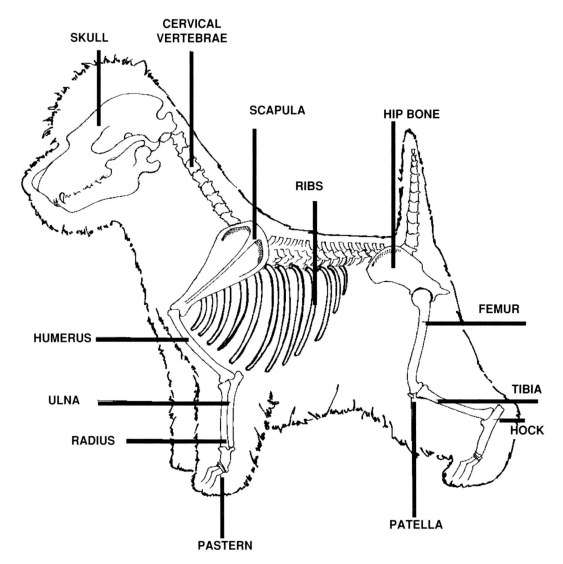

SKULL

CERVICAL
VERTEBRAE

SCAPULA

HIP BONE

RIBS

FEMUR

HUMERUS

ULNA

TIBIA

HOCK

RADIUS

PATELLA

PASTERN

ANATOMY OF THE WEST HIGHLAND WHITE TERRIER

withers, whereas in America the Standard states that males should be eleven inches, and females should be about one inch less. However, it is generally accepted in the UK that males should be about 18 lbs in weight, with females in the order of 15 lbs. This difference in weight is due to the male of the species being slightly larger and having heavier bone. The male and the female should be easy to distinguish just by looking at them – the male obviously looking masculine and the bitch appearing feminine. However, first and foremost, a Westie should be true to type, be of correct character, and have balance. If the dog moves correctly, it must be built correctly. I can recall being told this many years ago by an old terrier man. He said these are the prerequisites of any breed, and if you followed them, you would not go far wrong. How true this has proved to be! I have always tried to keep these points in mind, and to date, I am pleased to say they have stood me in good stead. A general guide to a well-balanced dog is: the length of back from tail to withers should be equal to the length of neck from occiput to withers, and from floor to withers. As in most terriers, the length of back to height fits snugly into a square box.

THE ENGLISH BREED STANDARD

GENERAL APPEARANCE Strongly built; deep in chest and back ribs; level back and powerful quarters on muscular legs and exhibiting in a marked degree a great combination of strength and activity.

CHARACTERISTICS Small, active, game, hardy, possessed of no small amount of self-esteem with a varminty appearance.

TEMPERAMENT Alert, gay, courageous, self-reliant but friendly.

HEAD AND SKULL Skull slightly domed; when handled across forehead presents a smooth contour. Tapering very slightly from skull at level of ears to eyes. Distance from occiput to eyes slightly greater than length of foreface. Head thickly coated with hair, and carried at right angle or less, to axis of neck. Head not to be carried in extended position. Foreface gradually tapering from eye to muzzle. Distinct stop formed by heavy, bony ridges immediately above and slightly overhanging eye, and slight indentation between eyes. Foreface not dished nor falling away quickly below eyes, where it is well made up. Jaws strong and level. Nose black and fairly large, forming smooth contour with rest of muzzle. Nose not projecting forward.

EYES Set wide apart, medium in size, not full, as dark as possible. Slightly sunk in head, sharp and intelligent, which, looking from under heavy eyebrows, impart a piercing look. Light coloured eyes highly undesirable.

EARS Small, erect and carried firmly, terminating in a sharp point, set neither too wide nor too close. Free from any fringe at top. Round pointed, broad, large or thick ears or too heavily coated with hair most undesirable.

MOUTH As broad between canine teeth as is consistent with varminty expression required. Teeth large for size of dog, with regular scissor bite, i.e. upper teeth closely overlapping lower teeth and set square to the jaws.

NECK Sufficiently long to allow proper set on of head required, muscular and gradually thickening towards base allowing neck to merge into nicely sloping shoulders.

FOREQUARTERS Shoulders sloping backwards. Shoulder blades broad and lying close to chest wall. Shoulder joint placed forward, elbows well in, allowing foreleg to move freely, parallel to axis of body. Forelegs short and muscular, straight and thickly covered with short, hard hair.

BODY Compact. Back level, loins broad and strong. Chest deep and ribs well arched in upper half presenting a flattish side appearance. Back ribs of considerable depth and distance from last rib of quarters as short as compatible with free movement of body.

HINDQUARTERS Strong, muscular and wide across top. Legs short, muscular and sinewy. Thighs very muscular and not too wide apart. Hocks bent and well set in under body so as to be fairly close to each other when standing or moving. Straight or weak hocks most undesirable.

FEET Forefeet larger than hind, round, proportionate in size, strong, thickly padded and covered with short harsh hair. Hindfeet are smaller and thickly padded. Under surface of pads and all nails preferably black.

TAIL 12.5-15 cms (5-6 ins) long, covered with harsh hair, no feathering, as straight as possible, carried jauntily, not gay or carried over back. A long tail undesirable, and on no account should tails be docked.

GAIT/MOVEMENT Free, straight and easy all round. In front, legs freely extended forward from shoulder. Hind movement free, strong and close. Stifle and hocks well flexed and hocks drawn in under body giving drive. Stiff, stilted movement behind and cow hocks highly undesirable.

COAT Double coated. Outer coat consists of harsh hair, about 5 cms (2 ins) long, free from any curl. Undercoat, which resembles fur, short, soft and close. Open coats most undesirable.

COLOUR White.

SIZE Height at withers approximately 28 cms (11 ins).

FAULTS Any departure from the foregoing points should be considered a fault and the seriousness with which the fault should be regarded should be in exact proportion to its degree.

NOTE Male animals should have two apparently normal testicles fully descended into the scrotum.

Reproduced by kind permission of the English Kennel Club.

THE AMERICAN BREED STANDARD

GENERAL APPEARANCE

The West Highland White Terrier is a small, game, well-balanced, hardy-looking terrier, exhibiting good showmanship, possessed with no small amount of self-esteem, strongly built, deep in chest and back ribs, with a straight back and powerful hindquarters on muscular legs, and exhibiting in marked degree a great combination of strength and activity. The coat is about two inches long, white in colour, hard, with plenty of soft undercoat. The dog should be neatly presented, the longer coat on the back and sides, trimmed to blend into the shorter neck and shoulder coat. Considerable hair is left around the head to act as a frame for the face to yield a typical Westie expression.

SIZE, PROPORTION, SUBSTANCE

The ideal size is eleven inches at the withers for dogs and ten inches for bitches. A slight deviation is acceptable. The Westie is a compact dog, with good balance and

substance. The body between the withers and the root of the tail is slightly shorter than the height at the withers. Short-coupled and well boned.
Faults – Over or under height limits. Fine-boned.

HEAD

Shaped to present a round appearance from the front. Should be in proportion to the body.
Expression – Piercing, inquisitive, pert.

Eyes – Widely set apart, medium in size, almond-shaped, dark brown in colour, deep set, sharp and intelligent. Looking from under heavy eyebrows, they give a piercing look. Eye rims are black.
Faults – Small, full or light coloured eyes.

Ears – Small, carried tightly erect, set wide apart, on the top outer edge of the skull. They terminate in a sharp point, and must never be cropped. The hair on the ears is trimmed short and is smooth and velvety, free of fringe at the tips. Black skin pigmentation is preferred.
Faults – Round-pointed, broad, large, ears set closely together, not held tightly erect, or placed too low on the side of the head.

Skull – Broad, slightly longer than the muzzle, not flat on top but slightly domed between the ears. It gradually tapers to the eyes. There is a defined stop, eyebrows are heavy.
Faults – Long or narrow skull.

Muzzle – Blunt, slightly shorter than the skull, powerful and gradually tapering to the nose, which is large and black. The jaws are level and powerful. Lip pigment is black.
Faults – Muzzle longer than the skull. Nose colour other than black.

Bite – The teeth are large for the size of the dog. There must be six incisor teeth between the canines of both lower and upper jaws. An occasional missing premolar is acceptable. A tight scissor bite with upper incisors slightly overlapping the lower incisors or level mouth is equally acceptable.
Faults – Teeth defective or misaligned. Any incisors missing or several premolars missing. Teeth overshot or undershot.

NECK, TOPLINE, BODY

Neck – Muscular and well set on sloping shoulders. The length of the neck should be in proportion to the remainder of the dog.
Faults – Neck too long or too short.

Topline – Flat and level, both standing and moving.
Faults – High rear, any deviation from above.

Body – Compact and of good substance. Ribs deep and well arched in the upper half of rib, extending at least to the elbows, and presenting a flattish side appearance.
Back ribs of considerable depth, and distance from last rib to upper thigh as short as compatible with free movement of the body. Chest very deep and extending to the elbows with breadth in proportion to the size of the dog. Loin short, broad and strong.
Faults – Back weak, either too long or too short. Barrel ribs, ribs above elbows.

TAIL

Relatively short, with good substance, and shaped like a carrot. When standing erect it is never extended above the top of the skull. It is covered with hard hair without feather, as straight as possible, carried gaily but not curled over the back. The tail is set on high enough so that the spine does not slope down to it. The tail is never docked.
Faults – Set too low, long, thin, carried at half-mast, or curled over back.

FOREQUARTERS

Angulation: Shoulders – Shoulder blades are well laid back and well knit at the backbone. The shoulder blade should attach to an upper arm of moderate length, and sufficient angle to allow for definite body overhang.
Faults – Steep or loaded shoulders. Upper arm too short or too straight.

Legs – Forelegs are muscular and well boned, relatively short, but with sufficient length to set the dog up so as not to be too close to the ground. The legs are reasonably straight, and thickly covered with short hard hair. They are set in under the shoulder blades with definite body overhang before them. Height from elbow to withers and elbow to ground should be approximately the same.

Faults – Out at elbows, light bone, fiddle-front.

Feet – Forefeet are larger than the hind ones, are round, proportionate in size, strong, thickly padded; they may properly be turned out slightly. Dewclaws may be removed. Black pigmentation is most desirable on pads of all feet and nails, although nails may lose coloration in older dogs.

HINDQUARTERS

Angulation: Thighs are very muscular, well angulated, not set wide apart, with hock well bent, short, and parallel when viewed from the rear.

Legs – Rear legs are muscular and relatively short and sinewy.
Faults – Weak hocks, long hocks, lack of angulation. Cow hocks.

Feet – Hind feet are smaller than front feet, and are thickly padded. Dewclaws may be removed.

COAT

Very important and seldom seen to perfection. Must be double-coated. The head is shaped by plucking the hair, to present the round appearance. The outer coat consists of straight, hard white hair, about two inches long, with shorter coat on neck and shoulders, properly blended and trimmed to blend shorter areas into furnishings, which are longer on stomach and legs. The ideal coat is hard, straight and white, but a hard straight coat which may have some wheaten tipping is preferable to a white fluffy or soft coat. Furnishings may be somewhat softer and longer but should never give the appearance of fluff.
Faults – Soft coat. Any silkiness or tendency to curl. Any open or single coat, or one which is too short.

COLOR

The color is white, as defined by the breed's name.
Faults – Any coat color other than white. Heavy wheaten color.

GAIT

Free, straight and easy all round. It is a distinctive gait, not stilted, but powerful,

with reach and drive. In front the leg is freely extended forward by the shoulder. When seen from the front the legs do not move square, but tend to move toward the centre of gravity. The hind movement is free, strong and fairly close. The hocks are freely flexed and drawn close under the body, so that when moving off the foot the body is thrown or pushed forward with some force. Overall ability to move is usually best evaluated from the side, and topline remains level.
Faults – Lack of reach in front, and/or drive behind. Stiff, stilted or too wide movement.

TEMPERAMENT

Alert, gay, courageous and self-reliant, but friendly. Faults – Excess timidity or excess pugnacity.

Reproduced by kind permission of the American Kennel Club.

   Whilst dealing with the Breed Standards, I feel it would be worthwhile including a relatively new international Standard which has been compiled. This standard has been produced by the Federation Cynologique International and is generally referred to as the FCI Standard.

THE FCI STANDARD

GENERAL APPEARANCE

Strongly built, deep in chest and back ribs, level back and powerful quarters on muscular legs and exhibiting in a marked degree a great combination of strength and activity.

CHARACTERISTICS

Small, active, game, hardy, possessed of no small amount of self-esteem with a varminty appearance.

TEMPERAMENT

Alert, gay, courageous, self-reliant but friendly.

HEAD AND SKULL

Skull: slightly domed, when handled across forehead presents a smooth contour. Tapering very slightly from skull at level of ears to eyes. Distance from occiput to eyes slightly greater than length of foreface.
Head: thickly coated with hair, and carried at right angle or less to axis of neck. Head not to be carried in extended position.
Foreface: gradually tapering from eye to muzzle. Distinct stop formed by heavy, bony ridges immediately above and slightly overhanging eyes.
Foreface: not dished nor falling away quickly below eyes, where it is well made up.
Jaws: strong and level.
Nose: black and fairly large, forming smooth contour with rest of muzzle. Nose not projecting forward.

EYES

Set wide apart, medium in size, not full, as dark as possible. Slightly sunk in head, sharp and intelligent, when looking from under heavy eyebrows, impart piercing look. Light coloured eyes highly undesirable.

EARS

Small, erect and carried firmly, terminating in a sharp point, set neither too wide nor too close. Hair short and smooth (velvety), should not be cut. Free from any fringe at the top. Round-pointed, broad, large or thick ears or too heavily coated with hair most undesirable.

MOUTH

As broad between canine teeth as is consistent with varminty expression required. Teeth large for size of dog, with regular scissor bite, i.e. upper teeth closely overlapping the lower teeth and set square in jaws.

NECK

Sufficiently long to allow proper set on of head required, muscular and gradually thickening towards base allowing neck to merge into nicely sloping shoulders.

FOREQUARTERS

Joint placed forward, elbows well in, allowing foreleg to move freely, parallel to axis of body. Forelegs short and muscular, straight and thickly covered with short, hard hair.

BODY

Compact. Back level, loins broad and strong. Chest deep and ribs well arched in upper half presenting a flattish side appearance. Back ribs of considerable depth and distance from last rib of quarters as short as compatible with free movement of body.

HINDQUARTERS

Strong, muscular and wide across top. Legs short, muscular and sinewy. Thighs very muscular and not too wide apart. Hocks bent and well set in under body so as to be fairly close to each other when standing or moving. Straight or weak hocks most undesirable.

FEET

Forefeet larger than hind, round, proportionate in size, strong, thickly padded and covered with short harsh hair. Hindfeet are smaller and thickly padded. Under surface of pads and all nails preferably black.

TAIL

5 to 6 inches long, covered with harsh hair, no feathering, as straight as possible, carried jauntily, not gay or carried over back. A long tail undesirable, and on no account should tails be docked.

GAIT/MOVEMENT

Free, straight and easy all round. In front legs freely extended forward from shoulder. Hind movement free, strong and close, stifle and hocks well flexed and hocks drawn under body giving drive. Stiff, stilted movement behind and cow hocks highly undesirable.

COAT
Double coated. Outer coat consists of harsh hair, about 5 cms (2 ins) long, free from curl. Undercoat, which resembles fur, short, soft and close. Open coats most undesirable.

COLOUR
White.

SIZE
Height at withers approximately 28 cms (11 ins).

FAULTS

Any departure from the foregoing points should be considered a fault and the seriousness with which the fault should be regarded should be in exact proportion to its degree.

Note: Male animals should have two apparently normal testicles fully descended into the scrotum.

This standard was approved by the General Assembly on the 23rd and 24th June 1987 in Jerusalem.

INTERPRETATION

SIZE

If a Westie is the wrong size it can be as important as any other fault, as it can spoil the overall impression of the dog. In fact, there are few Westies that are too big, but when this occurs it usually results in coarseness. It cannot be right to see a Westie that is close to a Wire Fox Terrier in size. There are those in the breed who interpret the expression 'a stallion of a dog' as meaning a large dog. This is a complete misinterpretation of the word 'stallion' in this context. The dictionary states that a stallion is a horse with two fully descended testicles; there is no mention of the size of the horse. A 'stallion of a dog' is one which is strong in bone, carries itself with its head held high, and is full of confidence. A stallion knows he is the best and shows it, he has that certain aura. Similarly, a Westie which is too small and below the size stipulated in the Breed Standard is usually lacking in bone and looks quite weedy. We should all aim for the size as laid down in the Breed Standard.

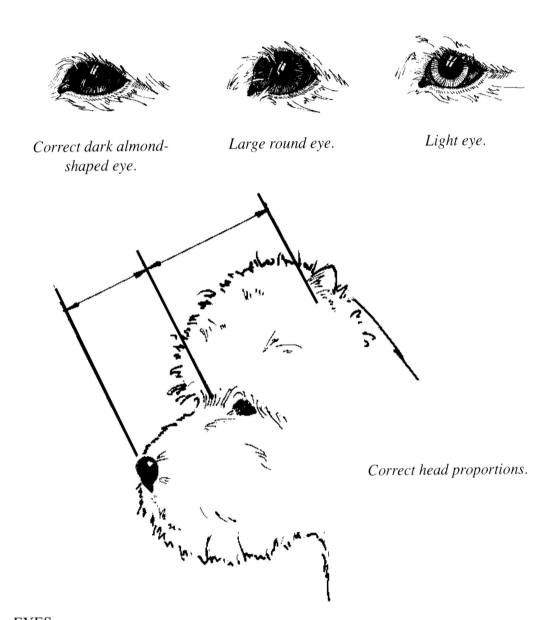

Correct dark almond-shaped eye.

Large round eye.

Light eye.

Correct head proportions.

EYES

The eyes should be almond-shaped and very dark brown in colour. A dog should be faulted if it has large, round or bulbous eyes. Equally the eyes must not be too small. The aim is for the eyes to give an intelligent, piercing expression. They should be set wide apart, and eyes which are light in colour are most objectionable.

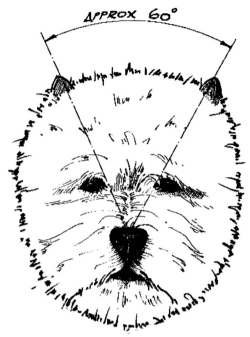

Correctly placed ears.

Ears set too close.

Ears set too low.

Ears too large.

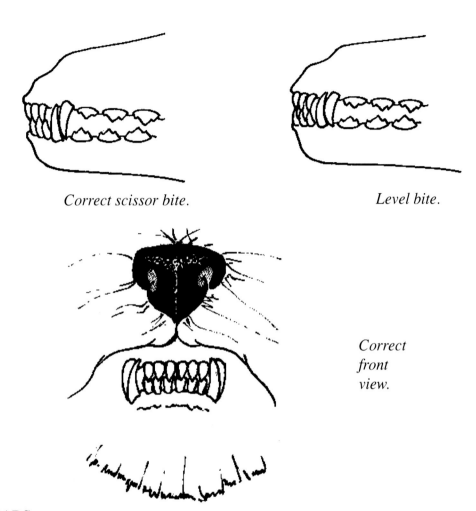

Correct scissor bite.

Level bite.

Correct front view.

EARS

One of the worst faults is to see soft ears on a dog, which flop up and down when it is on the move. This also applies to drop ears. The ears should be pricked up at all times. Ears which are too large for the size of the dog or ears that are set too close together distort the shape of the head, and ears that are set too low on the head give the dog a donkey-like appearance.

MOUTH

The teeth should meet in a regular scissor bite, and therefore an undershot or an overshot jaw should be faulted. There should be six incisor teeth in both upper and

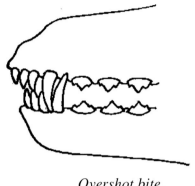

Overshot bite.

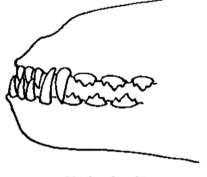

Undershot bite.

lower jaw, and the overall effect should be strong and powerful. On the Continent, and particularly in Germany, judges like to check the number of premolars – there should be six in the upper jaw and eight in the lower jaw – and a dog will be faulted if it has any missing teeth. In the UK we do not concern ourselves too much about the pre molars since the prerequisite of any terrier is to kill its prey, and therefore we are much more concerned that it should have a correct scissor bite in order to do the job of work it was originally bred for. When I was judging in Germany I was once asked what we did in the UK about missing premolars. I replied: "Nothing". The German exhibitor objected to this saying that the Westie was a hunting dog, and how would it be able to carry its prey with missing premolars. My answer was: "Have you ever tried to take a kill away from a terrier?"

NECK

Westies should be faulted for over-elongated necks – for being 'swan necked', as it is commonly known. If the neck is too short in length, it is usually because the dog is incorrect in shoulder. The neck should not be too thin or too thick. Quite often you see a Westie with a short, thick neck, and this is usually termed being 'stuffy' in neck.

FOREQUARTERS

A Westie should not be too narrow in front, appearing as though both legs come out of the same hole. It should not be too wide in front, fiddle-shaped or splay-legged. The feet should not turn out too far; in fact if they turn out a little, it is acceptable.

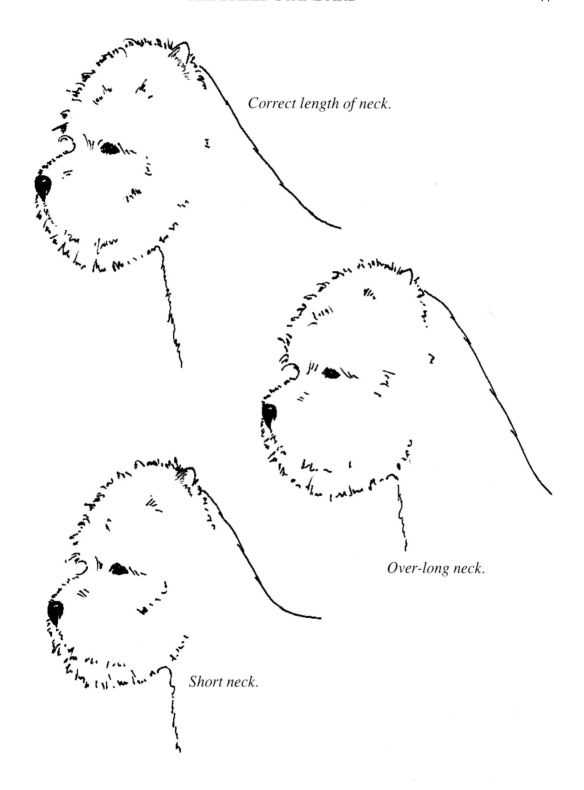

Correct length of neck.

Over-long neck.

Short neck.

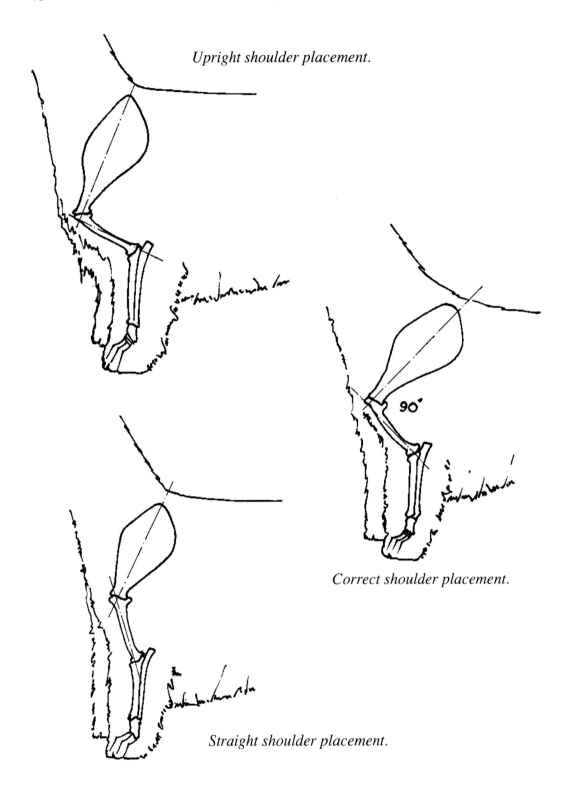

Upright shoulder placement.

90°

Correct shoulder placement.

Straight shoulder placement.

Correct front.

Narrow front.

Wide front.

Toeing in.

There is a misconceived idea which is prevalent, especially in America, that a Westie should have the front paws turning out in order for it to dig. This implies that when a Westie goes to ground, it digs the soil out along the side of its body. However, if this was the case, the rear legs would have to be placed together in order to create the necessary space. This would cause the dog to be unbalanced, because a Westie digs with both front legs at the same time in a cycling motion, and its hind legs are spread apart to give it balance and anchorage. The soil is then scooped through the gap between its rear legs. Every now and again, the dog will back out of the hole, and scoop the soil away with both front legs to avoid being locked in. If you are unsure of this just watch and study a dog going to ground: it does not have to be a Westie – all dogs dig in the same way.

BODY

The Westie should not have barrel ribs; the rib-cage should be similar to a heart shape. This is why you must never say that a Westie has a good spring of rib: if it has, then it is incorrect. The back should be level with no dipping behind the shoulders, no falling away in front of the tail, and no sloping from shoulder to tail. The rump should not rise above the height of the shoulders.

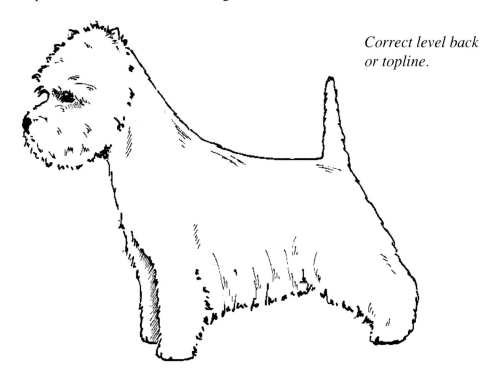

Correct level back or topline.

Dipping behind shoulder and too high in rump. This is due to incorrect rear angulation of hip joint, being straight in stifle and too long in hock.

Back sloping from shoulder to tail. This is mainly due to being too straight in shoulder (this also makes the neck too short) and being too long in hock.

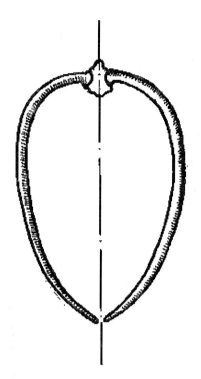

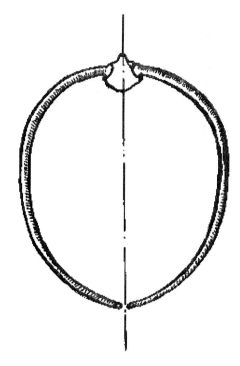

*Correct slab-sided
ribcage of the Westie.*

*Incorrect barrel ribcage,
giving the spring of rib that
is more associated with the
Scottish Terrier.*

HINDQUARTERS

Cow hocks should be faulted, and so should a dog that is too high in the hocks: this
makes the stifle too short and straight, and therefore lacking in angulation. The
hocks should be set straight under the body when viewed from the rear. Toeing in or
plaiting while on the move not acceptable.

TAIL

The tail should be a nice carrot shape, i.e. thick at the base and gradually tapering to
a point at the tip. A tail that is short in length, too long or too thin should be faulted.
The tail should be square on top, and never tucked down between the legs and under
the body. The tail must not be low-set or carried at half-mast. A tail with a bend like
a sickle is not acceptable.

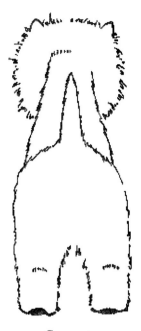

Correct rear.

Narrow rear.

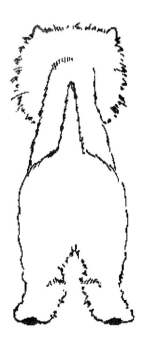

Cow-hocked.

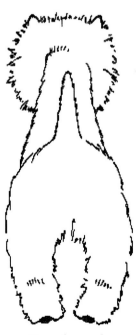

Bow-legged.

Correct tail set and carriage.

Gay tail.   *Low-set tail.*   *Half-mast tail.*

COAT

A Westie that has a single outer coat with no undercoat is not typical of the breed. The outer coat should be harsh, straight and lying flat against the body, with a close fur-like undercoat. The coat is designed to protect the dog against all weather conditions: the outer coat is to stop rain or snow getting through to the skin, and the undercoat is for warmth. An open coat is unacceptable. The harsh outer coat is also to protect the dog against having its coat torn out by bramble when it is running through the undergrowth.

Chapter Four

SELECTING
A PUPPY

Whether you are choosing a dog as a pet or for the show ring, initially the same rules apply. First and foremost, temperament is the top priority. Once you are confident that a pup is friendly and out-going, and is not unduly suspicious or nervous, you can then start looking more closely at any other attributes the puppy may have. If you are looking for a pet puppy and you are buying from a recognised breeder-exhibitor, you are unlikely to have much choice in which pup you can have. The breeder will already have selected any puppies of show potential, either for themselves or to go to show homes. However, if you are lucky enough to be offered a choice, then look for the puppy that comes to you happily, one that obviously enjoys being with humans, and especially with strangers. Check that the puppy has no obvious deformities and that it appears fit and well, with no evidence of badly running eyes, bald patches on its skin, mucus running from its nose, or a discharge from one or both ears. If you are satisfied that the puppy has none of these problems, then go ahead and buy it, on the understanding that you intend taking the pup to the vet for a health check.

The great majority of breeder-exhibitors will only ever use dogs of high quality and good pedigrees in their breeding programmes. However, it is an unfortunate fact that not all the pups that are born are ideal specimens for the show ring. When you

Ch. Olac Moonpilot, Supreme Champion-to-be, at fourteen weeks.

are dealing with livestock, anything can happen, and that is equally true whether you are breeding dogs, cats, farm animals, wild animals or even human beings – there are no guarantees. You can have the best dog and the best bitch in the world, put them together, and you can still end up with very average quality specimens. None of these puppies may be suitable for showing, but they are perfectly good pedigree puppies for the pet owner. Obviously, the challenge for the breeder-exhibitor is to find the right combination of genes to produce puppies which are superior in quality to previous litters they have bred – and, hopefully, to produce a puppy which is better than any bred by their contemporaries. This is what competition is all about.

When the litter starts to get on their feet and move around, at approximately three to four weeks, both their ears and eyes will be open and you will now notice their teeth are also making an appearance. This is the beginning of quite an eventful period in their little lives; you can see their personalities developing daily. It is a big decision selecting which puppy you want to keep for showing, and it should not be reached too hastily. Study all the puppies carefully, looking at their movement, and how they carry themselves. Observe their temperament, watching their reactions in relation to their litter mates. I know the Westie, like all dogs, is a pack animal, but in every pack there is a leader. I always try to pick the leader, because I know this is the one which will have the confidence, and the presence, and will therefore show to the

Ch. Olac Moondrift at seven months.

best of its ability. A really top quality show puppy should pick itself for you; it will stand out like a ray of sunshine and hit you between the eyes. Every time you go to look at the litter, there it will be, standing out from the rest. You will always be attracted to the same one, and you will find that you have eyes for no other.

When the puppies are about seven weeks of age, I like to handle each puppy on the grooming table. I start by giving the puppy a little brush down, and then give it a practice at standing, going over the puppy by feeling the shoulder placement, thickness of bone, whether it has good hocks, and a nice, short tail with good set-on. It is between the ages of seven and eight weeks that I start deciding which puppies to sell as pets, and those I want to run on for longer because of their potential. Obviously, if I find a puppy with serious faults, as far as showing is concerned, such as a poor head, straight shoulders, a bad front, poor movement, or incorrect tail carriage, then it must go as a pet. I tend to be very selective, and any puppy that I keep for its show potential must move well and appear generally well balanced. I am also very particular that the puppies that are not going to make the grade are only sold to suitable pet homes.

This is a good time to do a little trimming, starting round the neck, using thinning scissors. Then you can trim the tips of the ears, and shape the tail, using straight scissors. You may find it necessary to get someone to hold the puppy when you first begin trimming. Obviously, you must take great care when you are doing this, as you do not want to remove chunks of coat which should remain. This is all part of the learning process, for both you and the puppy, and with plenty of encouragement the pup will soon get used to being handled. This is also the time to start leash training your puppy. Obviously, this needs to be done in the house or the garden, as the puppy will not yet have received its inoculations. I never use a collar and leash at this stage; instead I begin by using a slip nylon leash, which is nice and light. If you use a collar you may well find that it will break the coat and leave a mark round the neck – definitely not what is required when you are trimming for the show ring. The best way to get a puppy used to having something round its neck is to put the leash on, and then let the pup roam around on its own – although under supervision. The pup will eventually accept this, and then you can begin to hold the other end of the leash. If you build this routine up gradually, it does not torment the puppy, and it will be perfectly happy to be on a leash when you are ready to take it out. Remember, it will have enough to contend with, seeing traffic and hearing all those strange noises, without the added fear of having a noose placed round its neck for the first time.

Chapter Five

BREEDING

After buying and showing your first Westie, I will guarantee that the bug will have bitten, and the next step in your programme will be to try to produce your own show puppy and start your own breeding line. This is a natural progression, and in many ways it makes sense, especially as you will have realised by now that most breeders will not sell you their very best stock – they will, more often than not, wish to keep these specimens for themselves. However, by contacting a recognised breeder you will at least be starting with reliable stock, and with a recognised pedigree from which to continue. This does not necessarily mean you will start breeding Champions from the word go – lucky you, if you achieve this! But there is a lot of learning that needs to be undertaken before you can establish your own line. You will need to find out about all the dogs that feature in your dog's pedigree; you need to find out what type these were, and whether you like the type and want, as near as possible, to attempt to emulate it. This research can be quite complicated, and you may find it helpful to look back over photographs of past Champions. The West Highland White Terrier Club of England has a special photo album: I found this very helpful in my early days in the breed, and I still use it as a reference if I come across a dog that I am not familiar with. One thing I can promise you is that, once you become involved in this new hobby, you will become absolutely fascinated by it.

The newcomer to the breed may well look round at the established breeders, who continually produce top quality pups, and it must seem relatively easy. Let me dispel that idea from your mind, here and now. As in all things, people with experience always seem to have the knack of making it look easy. When you become involved in breeding animals you discover the numerous pitfalls and setbacks, and there are times when you wish you had never started. However, there is also the day when you bring out your own home-bred puppy and start winning, and then it all seems worthwhile. If you have that extra good fortune you may go on to produce a really top dog, and then you will understand the true satisfaction that comes from all that hard work and heartache.

There is one fact which has stood the test of time, and should be remembered by all breeders: the strength of any kennel lies in the strength of its bitches. It is therefore important to strive for quality and soundness in your bitches. You can always have the pick of any dog in the country for stud, but unless you have quality bitches you will always lag behind the top producers. When I am planning my breeding programme, I personally prefer to line-breed. That means putting two animals together which have some similarities in their pedigrees; they should not be too closely related, but I like to have one line on the pedigree which ties up. I think in this way you have more idea predicting the type of Westie you will end up with, without doubling up too closely on any faults which may be in the lines – with the exception of the one line, and hopefully there will not be too many faults there. Obviously, it is important to know the faults in any line, and the degree of severity of these faults. If you are aware of any serious faults, you must be honest with yourself, and with others, and not allow that particular animal to be used as breeding stock. This is the only way to eliminate serious faults from the breed. For example, I would never breed from a dog which had a bad mouth. I have been lucky in never having had this problem in my line, but I know there are those who have, and yet they have still continued breeding from this stock. You can delude yourself into believing that you can breed this fault out in two or three generations, but, as sure as eggs is eggs, the problem will arise again, and I guarantee that it will happen when you least expect it.

Some people prefer to have a complete out-cross when they are planning a mating. This means that the pedigrees of both the sire and the dam bear no relationship to each other whatsoever. I am not in favour of this type of mating on a permanent basis, but I do appreciate that there is a time when it is necessary in order to introduce new blood to a line. The danger in line-breeding is that a line will become too closely in-bred and it will start to weaken. However, there are risks in out-crossing, too, as you never know what other faults you are going to bring into your

Ch. Olac Halfmoon Of Olac: produced two Champions in the same litter.

Ch. Olac Moonraker: proved to be an outstanding sire.

line, and you have no idea what type you are going to end up with. Complete in-breeding is another method practised by one or two breeders. In order to be successful with this method, you must be absolutely sure of your facts relating to the breeding stock, and you must be completely confident that there are no deep-rooted inherent faults in their lines. I must say, I find it hard to accept this method, because you are always in danger of compounding any problem or problems, and the fault will keep rearing its ugly head in successive generations. Personally, it is a practice which scares me to death, and it is not a path I would consider following.

When you have decided on what type of breeding programme you wish to follow, and you have a good quality bitch that you want to breed with, the next step is to select a suitable stud dog. In order to do this, you must, first of all, make an honest assessment of your bitch and decide which are her weaker points and where improvements can be made. Then you need to look for a male that excels in these departments, but is not too weak in other areas. When you have located a suitable dog, ask the owner for a copy of the dog's pedigree, and enquire if the dog is available for stud work, and what the terms are. I would suggest you make sure the full terms are in writing before taking your bitch for mating, and also make sure you receive a receipt for your money with these terms written on it. I have recently heard of one or two very unpleasant situations that have developed over dealings with stud dogs; so if you proceed with caution, you will be covered, and there should be no misunderstandings. It should not matter how far away the dog lives, or to whom it belongs; the important consideration is that it must be right for your bitch. I have said it before, and I will say it again: the whole object of the exercise is to try and improve the breed as a whole. Naturally, there are no guarantees when you are dealing with livestock, and inevitably you are going to have disappointments somewhere along the way. You can bring the finest dog and bitch in the world together, and still end up with utter rubbish. In order to be successful, everything has to gel, and for this you need an element of luck as well as good planning. But when it does come right, oh boy, what a feeling and sense of achievement you will have! However, if the litter fails to meet your expectations, do not fall into the trap of blaming the stud dog; remember, it takes two to tango, and you just have to put any setbacks down to experience.

If you are starting from scratch with a puppy bitch, she will probably come into season when she is six months of age, although there is no hard and fast rule for this. The first season could occur at any time up to twelve months, and the bitch will usually come into season every six months from then onwards. I do not like breeding from a bitch under fifteen months of age. In fact, I usually wait until the third season before planning a litter. This gives the bitch the chance to mature and develop properly. However, before mating a bitch of any age, you must make sure that she is fit and well. A bitch which is overweight may have trouble conceiving, or she may have problems at the time of whelping. When a bitch is coming into season the first signs are a swelling of the vulva, followed by a discharge of blood. Keep a careful watch for this first sign of blood, and then count eleven days from this, and you will have the approximate day when she will be ready for mating. A good test is to scratch the bitch's back near the base of her tail, and if she is receptive she will usually start curling her tail to one side. Another useful tip for detecting the right day for mating is to press the flesh between the anus and the vulva. If it feels hard then she is not ready, but if it is soft and spongy, she is receptive.

Do not over-breed from your bitch: as a general guideline, I would only breed from a bitch once a year. If circumstances dictate otherwise, you could breed on two consecutive seasons, but then the bitch must be rested for a full twelve months before mating takes place again. Rearing a reasonable-sized litter takes a lot out of a bitch, and if you do not rest her, you will only lose the quality in subsequent litters. A bitch needs the rest, along with good quality food, in order to pass on the nutrients for producing the bone and substance which make good healthy puppies. The English Kennel Club have recently introduced a rule on breeding bitches, where they refuse to register puppies born to bitches over eight years of age, and the maximum number of litters allowed from any one bitch is six. I am sure any responsible breeder would fully agree with this move. It was not before time that something was done to protect these bitches; I only hope the Kennel Club has the power to enforce it. There are not many unscrupulous breeders around, but they do exist, and both dogs and people should be protected from them.

Some years ago I arranged to take a bitch to be mated to a dog who belonged to someone that I thought was a very experienced breeder-exhibitor. In fact, it turned out to be lucky-dip time, for neither the owner or the dog seemed to have much idea of what the bitch was there for. The owner was most apologetic, and he was very quick to suggest Westie dogs were not very good at stud work; there was no suggestion that the dog, or its owner, could possibly share some of the blame. A good stud-keeper must know his dogs, and the dogs must be taught what is expected of them. I have had several stud dogs, and each one has known exactly what was required. It is all a matter of how you approach the task, and the way the young dog is introduced to stud work. The care you take over this will determine how good or bad a dog will be when it comes to serving bitches. I like to find a nice, experienced bitch for a puppy dog, when he is about ten months old. A bitch that has been bred from previously will be used to being held whilst the mating takes place, and this, in turn, helps to train a young dog to accept the procedure. There are two very good reasons why both the bitch and dog should be held during the mating: firstly, you do not want the dog to be damaged by a bitch who suddenly starts to leap around while the mating is taking place, and secondly, the owners of the bitch may have travelled a long way, and will be paying a stud fee, therefore, you must ensure that the bitch is being mated properly. When you are starting a young dog off with stud work, it is essential to have an unlimited amount of patience and to avoid losing your temper. Not all youngsters are fully aware of the correct mating procedure; they become so excited, jumping over the bitch's back like a spring lamb, trying to mate her from the wrong end, on her side – anywhere except the right place. While all this is going on, the bitch is usually standing there with a bemused look on her face, wondering what on earth is going on. All you need is time and patience, and with encouragement and guidance, the dog will eventually realise what is required. Of course, some males need no encouragement at all; these are the ones we say 'have been here before'. After this first experience, I do not use the dog for stud work again until after he is twelve months old. This allows him to mature and his bones to set, and by the time you are ready to use him again, you will know if his first bitch is in whelp. The big danger in using a puppy too extensively before this time, is that it can result in his front becoming too wide. I have even heard it said they can become weak on their back legs, although I have no proof of this. As with a brood bitch, a stud dog should be kept in a healthy, fit condition, and just as the brood bitch should not be carrying excess weight, you do not want the stud dog to be overweight either. I never feed the bitch or the dog before a mating; I find it makes the dog too lethargic, and both dog and bitch have been known to regurgitate their food at the time of mating. Therefore, it makes more sense to feed them both after the mating, when they can relax and enjoy their food, and have a drink of fresh, clean water.

There are one or two ways of telling if the bitch has conceived. After two weeks, look at her vulva: if it has not gone back to its normal size and is still enlarged, this is usually a good sign that she is in whelp. After four weeks her nipples will begin to go bright pink in colour and start enlarging; you may also see a slight sticky discharge. If, at any time, she has a badly discoloured discharge from her vagina, or in any way looks distressed, then take her to your veterinary surgeon right away for a check-up – you can never be too careful. When you are certain that the bitch is in whelp, you can start feeding her twice a day, not increasing the amount too much, but rather splitting her main meal into two meals: one feed in the morning and one in the evening. On one of these meals I also sprinkle some calcium powder, to help the formation of good strong bone in the puppies.

Now is the time for you to decide where you want your bitch to whelp her puppies. This should be somewhere away from any other dogs so that she is able to relax and

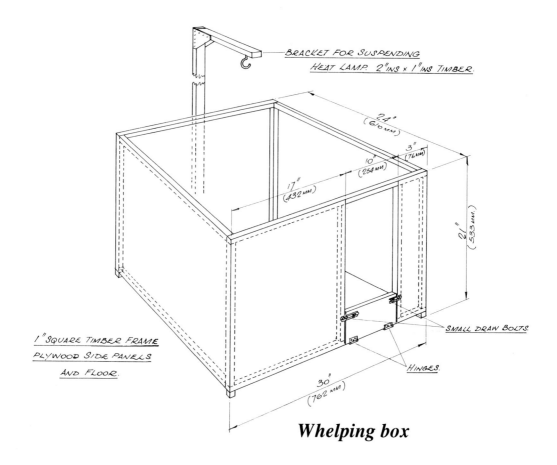

BRACKET FOR SUSPENDING
HEAT LAMP. 2"INS x 1"INS TIMBER.

24" (610MM)

3" (76MM)

10" (254MM)

17" (432MM)

21" (533MM)

1" SQUARE TIMBER FRAME
PLYWOOD SIDE PANELS
AND FLOOR.

SMALL DRAW BOLTS.

HINGES.

30" (762MM)

Whelping box

rest until the time arrives. We always use our spare room as a nursery. Whatever your choice, prepare the room in good time. A whelping box should be bought, or you can make your own, as long as you follow the recommended size for the breed (see diagram). I place a heater pad inside the box, passing the flex through a hole in the side of the box, so that the pups cannot chew it when they get older. For added warmth, and to ensure a constant temperature, I have a heat lamp above the whelping box. This is fixed to a bracket and fitted to the side of the box. It is best if you line the floor with thick layers of newspaper, and make sure you have plenty of spares in stock – we have friends who are under strict instructions not to throw away any newsprint! I would recommend you introduce your bitch to her new quarters about two weeks before the puppies are due; you will find she will relax and appreciate being away from the rest of the dogs. The recommended room temperature for the nursery should be approximately 21 degrees centigrade (70 degrees Farenheit), and it must be free from draughts. The time from mating to producing puppies is about nine weeks or sixty-three days, but it is not unknown for the litter to arrive two or three days early. If the bitch goes two or three days beyond the date she is due, or at any time appears distressed, you must take her to a veterinary surgeon without delay. The first sign that a bitch is beginning to go into labour is her refusal to eat a meal, usually about twelve hours before she goes into full labour. However, there is no hard and fast rule to this; some bitches do carry on eating. About ten days before the pups are born, the bitch will start preparing the nest by tearing up the paper in her whelping box. She may be fairly half-hearted in her 'nesting' to begin with, but the closer she gets to her time, the more obsessed she becomes with this activity. In the last couple of hours before her contractions start, she may become quite frenzied: tearing up the paper, and then trembling all over. Do not be alarmed by this, it is quite normal. In all probability, she will then settle down and have a good rest. After the rest she will start with the heavy panting, and again commence ripping up the paper to make a nest. This is very quickly followed by her first contractions, not too frequent at first but then gradually increasing until the water bag appears, followed by the first puppy. Leave the bitch to get on with things, and only interfere if you feel there is something wrong. However, you should always keep an eye on her, making sure that everything is going as nature intended. Some bitches like to be left alone during the whelping, while others seem desperate for you to be in attendance. Just play it by ear, and see how your bitch wants to manage things.

The normal way for a pup to be born is with the head coming first. However, occasionally you may get a puppy being born breeched, with the rear first, the head last, and the feet pointing down towards the underside of the bitch. Sometimes you may get a breech presentation with the legs facing upwards. In either of these situations, more often than not, the bitch will need some assistance because the head will be caught in the opening of the pelvis. In order to free the pup you will have to turn its whole body, while it is still inside the bitch. If this is necessary, you will need a bowl of warm water and some soap. Firstly, wet your hand, and then apply plenty of soap to your first and second fingers, then pass these two fingers, one either side of the puppy, and push them as far inside the bitch as you can. Grip the puppy, as near to the head as possible with these two fingers, and then grip the lower part of the pup with thumb, third and fourth finger. Now turn and pull the whole pup, and it should just slide away. If you are unsuccessful in freeing the pup, then obviously you will need to call the vet. Do not delay too long in reaching your decision to seek professional help, for time is of the essence. Hopefully there are some more pups still to be born, and you don't want them waiting too long.

When you have had to help to deliver a puppy, the bitch will often leave you to

*New-born puppy floating inside its membrane, showing the umbilical cord
with afterbirth still attached.*

remove the puppy from the bag it is born in. All you have to do is break open the
membrane from around its head and body, hold the pup in one hand, and with your
thumb and fingernails of this hand, tightly grip the umbilical cord approximately one
inch (25mm) away from its body. Then, using your other hand, bring your thumb
and finger to the other fingers, and again, gripping tightly with your nails, stretch
and break the cord. This method is far better than cutting with scissors, because the
very act of stretching closes the opening in the centre of the cord, and helps to seal it
as it breaks, thus helping to avoid any infection getting inside the tube. I usually
have a towel ready so that we can dry the puppy off right away, then give it back to
Mum, so she can snuggle up to it and and give it a good licking all over.

Once you are fairly sure the bitch has finished whelping, give her some warm milk containing approximately 5 mil. of liquid calcium; she will be ready for this. Make sure the bitch has plenty of milk of her own to pass on to the puppies, and keep a careful check that the pups are feeding from all stations. It has been known for them to leave two nipples alone, and these are usually the very back two, underneath the back legs. If this problem arises then you will have to express some of the milk from her; otherwise it will become very painful for her, and could lead to mastitis. Give her (and yourself) a few hours rest, then make arrangements to take her along to the vet for a check-up. If the bitch has done the whelping all on her own then you are never too sure if all the afterbirths have come away with each puppy. I like my bitches to have two injections, one to help clear any afterbirths left behind, and then an injection of antibiotics to help clear up any possible infection. It is advisable to have a bottle of liquid calcium and a syringe handy. I like to administer 10 mil. down the bitch's throat as soon as she has finished whelping, and 5 mil. per day thereafter, thus helping to prevent eclampsia setting in. Eclampsia is a condition where the bitch has passed on most of her body calcium to her pups, and she will start panting and shivering – and she may even try to attack her pups. If your bitch gets into this state at any time, then you must take her to the vet right away where she can have the calcium given intravenously. With this injection, the calcium gets into the system almost instantaneously, and she will quieten and recover very quickly. But always keep a sharp look-out for the tell-tale signs; some bitches are more prone than others to this condition, and it can be fatal.

For the first twenty-four hours the bitch should be restricted to a liquid diet; after that, I like to feed white meat, chicken or rabbit for about a week, and then gradually introduce red meat. I have had a bitch who would not drink milk on its own, so I tried mixing a little powdered drinking chocolate in with the milk, and bingo, it worked! During these first three or four days the bitch is very loath to leave her new family, so you will have to physically pick her up and put her outside to relieve herself. I know it is very tempting to start picking up the puppies to cuddle them, but many bitches do not like you doing this, so curb your natural inclinations by leaving them alone. It is only for a few days, until the bitch is satisfied they are all OK, and then it is quite in order for you to see them, and share in the enjoyment of having them around. There is a method in her madness, for you can now partake in looking after her pups, thus relieving her of some of the work. We call them dumb animals, but it makes you think, doesn't it?

Chapter Six

PUPPY REARING

The development of puppies is quite remarkable. It all happens so quickly, and it is always so fascinating to watch. I like to sex and weigh the pups when they are born, and I continue to weigh them for the first seven days so that I can keep a check on how well they are progressing. When they are three or four days old the vet removes the dewclaws on the front legs, and checks that there are no dewclaws on the hindlegs; if there are, these will also need to be removed. After the first week, I continue to weigh the pups on a weekly basis, keeping a record of all this information in a book. I find this very useful when I want to compare the progress of the present litter with previous litters I have reared. As a general rule, it is not unusual for a puppy to lose a little weight from its birth weight in the first twenty-four hours, but it should regain this within the next twenty-four hours. From then onwards the growth rate is phenomenal – it is almost as though someone is blowing them up with a bicycle pump! Most puppies will gain a number of ounces for the next few days, and some have been known to double their birth-weight in the first week.

There is a phenomenon, which all breeders dread, known as the Fading Puppy Syndrome. You may be one of the lucky people who have managed to avoid the loss of a puppy, or you may never have had a puppy that has displayed the symptoms relating to this condition, but no one that is dealing with livestock can afford to be complacent; just because you have not experienced a particular problem does not mean that you are never going to encounter it. When Fading Puppy Syndrome strikes, you are always trying to work out how and why it happened, and you feel an appalling sense of waste. It does not necessarily affect all the pups in a litter; it could be just one puppy that fails to thrive, and all the rest are perfectly fit and healthy. There are a number of possible causes for the death of a puppy in the first couple of weeks following its birth, even when it initially appears to be thriving. A normal puppy's defence against disease is dependent on the antibodies (colostrum) it receives from the bitch's milk the moment it starts feeding; and so a puppy is more likely to decline within the first three or four days if it is going to fall victim to this condition. The first sign is usually when the puppy stops suckling: it has the nipple in its mouth, but it seems unable to suck. The puppy makes sucking noises, and so it is easy to think that it is receiving nourishment. However, you will suddenly see it has lost a lot of body weight. This is one of the reasons why we like to weigh the puppies every day for the first few days, so that we can spot any ailing puppy as soon as the first signs appear.

If you have a new-born puppy which is unable to suckle, then you will need to hand-feed it. The puppy will need to be fed every two hours, night and day. There are specially designed feeding bottles which you can buy, but in an emergency, an eye-dropper will do the trick. I have seen many recommended recipes for hand-rearing, but I would recommend either of the following two, which have both been used with success:

One tablespoon of condensed milk *or* one tablespoon of milk made up with the formula used for babies.
One tablespoon boiling water.
A quarter-teaspoonful of honey.
A few drops of gripe water (A 200ml bottle contains 2.3mg Terpeneless Dill seed oil, 52.5mg sodium bicarbonate, plus water).

The following recipe was given a few years ago in a Westie newsletter, and was submitted by an American breeder. It works on the theory that prevention is better than cure, and if a puppy is treated in the following way it should prevent the onset of Fading Puppy Syndrome. As soon as a bitch is approaching parturition (expelling a whelp) make a five per cent glucose solution by mixing one teaspoonful of white corn syrup into four tablespoons boiled water. Add a few grains of sodium chloride (ordinary table salt) and a few grains of potassium chloride (salt substitute). This resembles a Ringers Glucose-Saline fluid but, of course, it cannot be used for subcutaneous or intravenous injection because it is not sterile. Put this solution into a

Litter of three puppies at approximately ten days old. Their eyes and ears are still closed, but the eyes will open within the next two or three days. The ears will open at about twenty-one days.

dropper bottle, and as soon as the puppy is dry and breathing normally, weigh it on a gram scale and give it five or six drops of the solution for each 100 grams body weight. It is best to administer the glucose drop by drop on to the puppy's tongue, rather than introducing it directly into the stomach by tube. Make sure the puppy has swallowed each drop before the next is given. After this initial feed, put the puppy with its dam for stimulation and warmth. Every four hours weigh the puppy, record its weight, and repeat the glucose, increasing the amount to as much as a full dropper or 1cc for each 100 grams body weight, if the puppy is not gaining weight. Continue this treatment until the puppy shows signs of gaining weight, then you can reduce the feeding times to every eight hours until it is forty-eight hours old. Never force a puppy to drink.

Many eminent men and women have tried to discover the cause of fading puppies, and infection, malnutrition, environmental factors, parasitic infestation, or inherited genes have all been investigated as possible causes. However, there is one important factor which is relatively easy to monitor, and that is temperature. New-born and young puppies need a constant warm environment with no draughts or dampness. The recommended room temperature is 21 degrees centigrade (70 degrees Fahrenheit), but you will still need to provide additional warmth in the form of a heat lamp, and possibly a heat-pad on the floor of the whelping box.

At approximately fourteen to sixteen days, the puppies' eyes will begin to open, and soon afterwards they will try to get up on their legs. This is the time when the litter is really becoming interesting; they are now more aware of the puppies around them, and play is the order of the day. The next development occurs at about twenty-one days when the puppies' ears start to open – I always love the look on their faces when they hear sounds for the first time! This is the time when I bring them down from the nursery into a room, which is just off the sitting room. I transfer the whelping box downstairs and put it into a play-pen, so that the puppies are contained within a certain area. This move means that the pups become used to all kinds of different noises: radio, television, telephone, they even get to hear the vacuum cleaner now and again! This is also the time to begin socialising them, allowing them to meet visitors when they come to the house. This is a good grounding for the future, especially if you have a puppy that looks as if it may be good enough for the show ring. I cannot stress too strongly how important these early days are in helping to form the character of your pups, whether they are to be sold as pets or are destined for the show ring.

The time you start weaning will depend on how many pups there are in the litter, and how well the bitch is looking after them. I have found the average age for weaning is between three and four weeks. However, there are always exceptions, and I always had to start weaning the litters from one particular bitch at two weeks of age, because, for some reason, her milk always dried up at about this time. I have never, before or since, seen puppies get up on their legs so quickly; they were driven by sheer hunger, and they chased that bitch all over the puppy run. Her attitude after two weeks of nursing seemed to be: "I have had the pups which you wanted me to have; now they are yours, and good luck to you!"

When I start weaning, I begin by feeding warm goat's milk with a little honey. A puppy is unable to support its own body at this age, so you will need to hold the puppy in your hand and let its nose just touch the milk. After a couple of tentative tastes, it will get the idea very quickly and start to lap. I repeat this procedure four times a day as the puppies are only small, and it will only take a little food to fill their tummies. A pup will soon tell you when it has had enough by fighting to get away from the dish. If you have a puppy who does not lap right away, coax it by dipping your finger in the milk, and let the liquid run into its mouth. For the first three days of weaning, milk is all that is required; then you can introduce the puppies to some porridge or baby's rusks (biscuits) crumbled up in milk. Make sure you do not forget the honey. Another option is a lightly scrambled egg, made up with plenty of milk.

When the puppies are about four weeks old, they will be ready for their first course of worming. For pups of this age I like to use a worming syrup, administered by syringe. It is important to follow the instructions carefully, and repeat the dose as instructed. There is another type of wormer, which can be used on dogs and puppies, which I have found to be first class. It is a non-sticky paste, and it comes in a tube similar to toothpaste. In most instances it is only available from the vet. All you have to do is squeeze the appropriate amount, according to your dog or pup's weight (against a scale which is provided) and then scoop the paste on to your finger and put it on the roof of the puppy's mouth. The advantage of this method is that the puppy cannot spit out the paste, and it is very easy to administer. Puppies should be wormed regularly, making sure that you follow the manufacturer's instructions, as puppies will never thrive if they are full of worms. It is also necessary to give your bitch a course of worming once she has finished feeding her pups, otherwise her health will diminish and she will never return to full fitness.

After approximately a week of feeding milky solids, you can begin to include meat in one of their daily meals. This should consist of either scraped meat or finely minced beef. I mash with a fork, and by adding boiling water, make a paste of it. Once the puppies have had a taste of meat there is rarely any problem from then onwards. As soon as they are accepting the meat happily, you can include another meat meal in their diet, so that their daily intake will be: a breakfast of porridge or

A fourteen week old puppy.

All puppies love to explore, and it is fascinating to observe their first experiences of the outside world.

rusks (biscuits), meat for lunch and dinner, and some warm milk before they are bedded down for the night. You can substitute boiled fish for one of these meat meals, if you want to introduce a change. This does not need not be expensive fish; coley is quite adequate, and the puppies do seem to enjoy it. I have found that they also like rice pudding, lightly scrambled egg, with milk, and a little grated cheese. Just ring the changes and give them a nice, balanced diet. When the puppies are about seven to eight weeks old they will require some roughage in their diet, so I begin mixing puppy terrier meal, or brown bread cut into small pieces, with their meat; I find this also helps to give them extra body.

While the bitch is feeding the pups she will normally take care of cleaning them. However, not all bitches are good mothers, so is advisable to keep checking that she is cleaning their rear ends. You will need to do this, anyway, as soon as you start weaning the pups on solid food, for she will stop cleaning them, and it will become your responsibility. Each puppy should be checked regularly to make sure it is not fouled up with its own faeces at the rear. If a puppy needs cleaning, use some cotton wool balls soaked in warm, soapy water. Do not forget to dry the pup after it has been cleaned. Obviously, as the puppies grow, you will need to increase the quantities of food, especially as they become less dependent on their mother. By the age of six weeks you can expect the puppies to be completely reliant on yourself for feeding and general care. The mother will not wish to be with her brood during the day, but she will still want to see them and have a play at some stage. The best time for this is the evening, and I have spent many a happy hour just watching their development – it makes better viewing than television and it never ceases to fascinate me.

The puppies will need to be vaccinated before you take them out further than your own garden. The vet will advise you when to start the course: it is usually between ten and twelve weeks, followed by the second inoculation two weeks later. Some vets also like to give a third inoculation at sixteen weeks for Parvovirus. My vet gives the first shot at ten weeks, which covers the major infectious diseases, followed by the second shot at twelve weeks for Leptaspirosis, which includes coverage for Parvovirus. Do not venture to take the puppy out for at least another three or four days after this second inoculation; give it time to go through the system and for the immunity to build up inside the pup.

Chapter Seven

ADULT FEEDING

Far be it from me to venture to tell you which food you should be giving your dog; I can only try to give advice, based on my own experiences. At the end of the day, you will find the type of feed which suits you, in terms of both convenience and finance. However, the most important consideration is to find out what suits your dog: what it likes to eat, and what keeps it fit and well. When you look round at the wide choice of dog diets available, it is no wonder that people become confused and do not know which way to jump. There are the all-in-one feeds, which are given dry or mixed with water. Because of the very low moisture content in these complete feeds, remember that it is imperative that your dog has a supply of clean, fresh water at all times. There are numerous brands of canned meats, and of biscuit-type meal, and, of course, there is the more traditional diet of tripe or fresh meat, always assuming that you have a cheap, reliable source of supply for this.

Today, the emphasis in America seems to be on the complete feed, known as Kibble. I also understand that this diet is becoming increasingly popular on the Continent. In fact, I have been reliably informed by one of the leading dog food manufacturers in the UK, that approximately 80 per cent of dog owners in America and on the Continent, feed their dogs a complete feed, and 20 per cent feed meat. In the UK, it is the exact opposite: 80 per cent use meat and 20 per cent use a complete feed. This proves, yet again, that traditions die hard in the UK, and it takes a little longer for new ideas to be absorbed. The British are loath to change just for the sake of change, and when breeders have been successful over a long period of time, they need a lot of convincing, plus concrete evidence, before they are ready to experiment with new ideas.

For the past few years I have fed my dogs on a top-quality canned meat, which I mix with a biscuit-type complete feed, using a ratio of one part canned meat to three parts complete feed. When this is measured out it corresponds to about 5oz of complete feed to one-third of a standard can of meat. As far as quantitity is concerned, you should always use your commonsense. Some dogs require more than others in order to maintain their body weight, and so it is important to assess each dog's individual requirements. I have found this diet of canned meat and complete feed to be excellent, both in terms of quality and convenience – the dogs certainly seem to thrive on it. They never have any problems with loose stools, and they maintain the right amount of body weight and, thank goodness, they keep fit and well. I know dogs are creatures of habit, and there are people who believe there is no need to change their diet, but I like to give my dogs an occasional change of food. I believe that they, like humans, get bored with the same food day in, day out. Tripe is a favourite with the dogs, and I also give them vegetables or rice left over from our own meals, mixed in with whatever we are feeding them that day. Occasionally my wife boils the carcass of a chicken or turkey, adding barley and vegetable stock, and I feed this to the dogs. They absolutely love this, and consider it a real treat. However, do be careful not to leave any bones in the broth. Chicken bones and chop bones are very brittle; they splinter when they are chewed, and the sharp slivers can be fatal to a dog.

The time of day that you feed your dog or dogs should fit in with your daily activities, but, as I have already said, dogs are creatures of habit and I would recommend that you feed at the same time each day. Try and get into a routine; you will find it much easier to cope, and it will certainly be appreciated by the animals. My dogs are fed once a day at approximately 4.30 pm, but I also like to give them a handful of dog biscuits or raw carrot each morning – a gap of twenty-four hours between meals seems an awfully long time, and I know some vets agree that it is too long for a dog to wait. The advantage of feeding items such as biscuits and carrot as the 'snack' meal is that they are good for the dog's teeth. A typical day's menu would be:

Morning: Three or four biscuits, or a raw carrot.
Evening: 5oz complete feed mixed with one-third of a can of standard meat.

I find the best way of measuring the complete feed is to give two good handfuls, rather than measuring the quantity with scales at every meal. The only exception to this feeding routine is on a very cold and frosty morning, when I feed a drink of warm milk, alongside the biscuits or carrot. My kennels have moderate heating, but when the temperature drops I find that the dogs appreciate having something warm in their stomachs at the beginning of the day.

Chapter Eight

TRIMMING

If you asked any exhibitor what aspect of caring for a Westie caused the most frustration and heartache, the vast majority would put trimming right at the top of their list. This is particularly the case for newcomers to the breed, who tend to learn a little here and a little there: they receive tips from a variety of people, it is often conflicting, and before they know where they are, total confusion has set in. In this chapter I will endeavour to dispel some of the mysteries of trimming, and hopefully it will help those who are climbing the wall in frustration over what seems to be an impossible task!

Time after time, I have heard people say: "If only I could trim, but it is the one thing I cannot do. You're the lucky one, you can do it." This statement implies I could trim dogs from the word go – rubbish! The number of hours I spent teaching myself is nobody's business, and unless you are prepared to put the time and effort into learning and perfecting the art of trimming, then you are always going to be an also-ran. I will be the first to admit that it helps to have an eye for trimming, but the same can be said about choosing a dog; you need to have an eye for balance, and one skill goes hand in hand with the other. Nobody is put on this earth with an instant ability to trim; it is an art which you have to work at, and continue to work at in order to perfect. More often than not, people are not prepared to put in the time and effort that is required in order to do the job properly; as the old saying goes: 'you only get out what you put in.' I have heard a number of people say they started getting their dog ready some two days prior to the day of the show, and yet they expect to compete on equal terms with others who are willing to work at getting their dogs ready well in advance of the show.

Inevitably, these are the people who moan that they cannot trim, and state that dogs should be judged on their construction, and not presentation. Their dogs are invariably a mass of coat, and often they are none too clean either. Nobody argues with the concept that a dog should be judged on its merits, but whichever way you view things, a dog should look the part, and presentation must have a say with the overall assessment. You can have two dogs of equal standing, but in the end the one with the better presentation must call the tune; we are, after all, competing in a 'dog show'. In fact, I would go so far as to say, that any dog shown by a so-called 'experienced' exhibitor, which is in a dirty, untrimmed condition, is an insult to the judge. The novice can be forgiven; they probably do not know any better, and they should be given help and encouragement. But there is no excuse for the experienced exhibitor. What would you say if you were attending a beauty parade, and an obviously attractive girl came along, with unkempt hair, no make-up and wearing a tatty costume? I gamble you would dismiss her from consideration, and you would probably make some rude remarks about her appearance. I will repeat myself and say we are competing in a dog show – a canine beauty parade. It therefore follows that the dogs should be presented to the very best of your ability, and surely, it is worth the time and effort if you care about your dog. There is nothing better than seeing a well-trimmed, sparkling white Westie hit the ring, and do its stuff – there is no doubt a Westie in this condition can certainly fill the eye.

In the following pages I will try, through text and pictures, to explain how to go about trimming your dog, with particular regard to the show ring, where you want your dog to look its best. For those people who just have a pet and want it to look as a Westie should, then I would suggest you contact a professional groomer in your area, who is able to do this for you. The dog will need to be trimmed every ten to twelve weeks, on average. Be sure that the professional groomer you patronise knows how to trim a Westie properly. Not all do. Ask your dog's breeder for the name of a qualified person. Too many groomers say they can trim Westies, but turn out badly clipped and unsightly results. Obviously, there will be exceptions to the rule, but unfortunately they are few and far between. Take my advice and go to an experienced Westie trimmer, wherever possible. However, if you feel you have the time, and you would like to have a go at trimming your own dog, then I hope this chapter will give you some insight and guidance on how to go about it. Good luck!

There is no mystique, no secret formulae, no magic potions, and no short-cuts in the art of trimming; it is just honest-to-goodness hard work, plus the determination

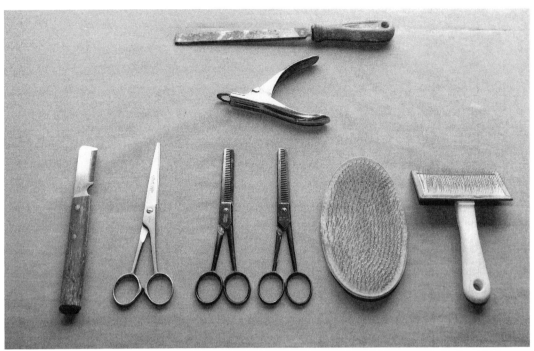

Grooming equipment.

to do the job properly. I say it is hard work, but in my case, I do not consider it a chore; maybe I am lucky because I actually enjoy doing it, and I don't mind spending the time it takes. Any dog which I am showing spends at least fifteen to twenty minutes a day on the grooming table. I start by giving the dog a good brush down, followed by trimming a little here and a little there, continually working the coat. If you trim in this way, you will eventually have a coat which is three or four layers thick. You are, in actual fact, removing a layer and making way for another new layer by rotating the coat on a continuous basis. I use the words 'rotating the coat', the Americans call it 'rolling the coat', but whatever you wish to call it, it is the only way to keep your dog in show condition, week in and week out. If you try to keep the same coat going without trimming in this way, I guarantee you will end up with what we commonly call a 'blown coat'. This is when the coat is dead. It goes very fine and lifeless, it has no depth to it, and it just blows around in the breeze. When the coat gets into this condition you have no alternative but to pull it all out, and then you have the prospect of waiting for weeks for it to grow in again.

Naturally, you will need some basic tools for doing the job. The first requirement is a good sturdy grooming table with a non-slippery surface, so that your dog will feel comfortable. A table with adjustable legs is advisable so you can adjust it to suit your height; there is nothing worse than working for only a couple of minutes and getting an aching back. There are grooming tables on the market, which come complete with wheels attached, and folding legs. These are ideal because they double as a trolley, and so you can transport your dog, in its travelling box, from the car to the show ground. Some people like to use a trimming stand which fixes to the table top; it has a leash hanging down from it which secures the dog. I, personally, do not like these. I much prefer to have the dog standing free: I find that it settles down much better without being restrained, but this is one for you to decide upon.

The type of brush I use all the time is a terrier palm brush or pin brush. This gets through the coat without damaging it. It is also ideal for using in the ring when you are showing. It fits nicely into the palm of the hand, hence the name, and it is flat and not bulky, so it is easy to slip into your pocket. Other exhibitors like using a slicker brush, but I find that this has a tendency to rake out too much of the undercoat, and it can also break the top coat. You will require at least two pairs of good-quality scissors. I find the thirty-two teeth thinning scissors are ideal – they are less likely to give you a sharp line in the coat when used correctly – and I also use a pair of sharp straight six-inch scissors. If you are trimming correctly, you should not use the scissors a great deal, but they are needed for the finishing touches, and therefore you should not skimp on the quality – besides they will give the greater length of service.

The dog's nails should be kept nice and short, and you can either use proper canine guillotine clippers, or regularly use a six-inch engineer's file, as I do. When you are using clippers it is all too easy to cut into the quick, especially if your dog has all-black nails, making it impossible to see how far the quick has grown. If you cut the quick it is very painful for the dog, and the nail can bleed quite a lot. If you use a file, as I suggest, there is no danger of filing into the quick – you will find the dog pulls away before you get that close. Filing the nails on a weekly basis takes only a few minutes, and it keeps them at the correct length; you will also find the quick receding back with the nail. If you fail to keep the nails short, your dog will start to look as if it is flat-footed, and it gives the impression that it is down on its pasterns. Similarly, you will give the same impression if you do not cut the hair fairly close, trimming just behind the last large pad on each paw.

As the Westie's coat does not moult in the same manner as other breeds, we have to actually hand-strip or pluck the dog's coat. When you are plucking, all you are doing is taking out the dead hair. This has to be done in order to stimulate the growth of new coat. Many people think that this process of trimming by plucking must be painful for the dog. However, if it is done correctly, this is not the case. In order to carry out this task many exhibitors use a stripping knife, but I prefer to use my finger and thumb. This is a method I have used since doing my first Westie trim; it suits me because I feel I have much greater control. However, it is important to use whichever method is most comfortable for you, and most to your liking. When you are stripping a dog, there is one rule that you should remember: if you decide to trim one part of the dog, then you must trim the identical part on the opposite side, on the same day. This is something which should become so much of a habit that you do it automatically. For example, if you trim one shoulder, then you must do the other shoulder at the same time, or if you trim one front leg, then you must trim the other front leg on the same day. Never trim one side on one day, and then leave the other side to do the next day. Even if you have all the very best intentions in the world, something could happen, so that you are unable to continue where you left off the previous day. Before you realise it, two or three days may have gone past before you get back to trimming that other shoulder or that other front leg. The result of this is that you end up with differing thicknesses and lengths of coat on various parts of the dog. This makes the coat very uneven, and the dog appears to be out of balance. Once you have got into this situation, you have a big problem, and it can take many weeks before you are able to rectify the situation. So be warned and always follow this rule.

I always rub a little loose chalk into the area I am about to trim – this gives me the ability to grip the hair better – and I always pull the coat in the same direction it grows. For the show dog there are areas which require closer trimming than others, for example, underneath the neck and down the chest, the side of the neck and over the shoulders. From a line level with the ears, on top of the neck, and over the withers, the hair should be left longer and thicker, running into the top of the back. The whole art of trimming revolves around the smooth blending from one section of the dog into the next; there should be no lines due to scissor marks or sharp corners. For example, the coat on the side of the neck should be short but longer on the top, so where the longer coat meets the shorter coat, there should be a gradual transformation from long to short. Where the neck hair meets the hair on the back, there must be no ridge or sharp corners, it should just flow from one to the other. The area underneath the neck and down the chest is a very tender section, so in order not to upset the dog unduly I use a combination of thinning scissors and a little gentle pulling.

When you are trimming, be careful not to work in one area all the time, or you will end up with holes in the coat. The method that some people adopt for hand-stripping is to lift the hair between finger and thumb in one hand, and then to pull the longer hairs with finger and thumb of the other hand. This is a method I do not much care for: in my estimation it is far too easy to fall into the trap of working in one area, and it is the easiest way to get holes, or a very unevenly trimmed coat. I much prefer to work with one hand, lifting the coat with my thumb with a brushing motion against the lay of the coat and away from my body. The good coat will spring back into position, leaving the dead hair still standing. With finger and thumb, grip these dead hairs in a pulling action on the return motion with your hand back towards the body. To all intents and purposes, it is the same action as plucking a chicken. By using this method I can work in a wider area, thus eliminating the possibility of putting any holes in the coat. This may sound complicated, but it is all done in the one movement, and once you get into the swing of it, it is quite easy. I am a naturally right-handed person, but, with practice over the years, I have managed to train myself to trim with either hand. I am sure you will also be able to train yourself to use both hands, with a bit of determination. It certainly makes the job much easier and less tiring.

Some Westie enthusiasts in America often like to leave a clump, or bib of hair sticking out from just above the breast bone and down between the front legs. This is intended to show that a dog has a good overhang of chest, and also indicates good shoulder placement. However, the Breed Standard does not stipulate that the Westie should have a keel, or large overhang of chest, and I have to disagree with American exhibitors on this point. I believe that it makes the dog look more like a Scottish Terrier, which has a completely different chest from that of the Westie. A Westie with the correct rib cage and shoulder angulation, with good layback of shoulder, as required in the breed, should not have a big overhang of chest. Generally speaking, the Scottish Terrier is unable to have the same layback of shoulder because of his large barrel rib-cage. Consequently it is much heavier, more upright in shoulder, and ultimately it is heavier in shoulder, thus producing a greater chest width and overhang. Therefore, why leave this clump of hair on a Westie, which gives the impression your dog is longer than it is? The Westie should be a sleeker animal altogether than the Scottish Terrier. Obviously, this is an area of some controversy, and doubtless it will provoke discussion for some time to come.

The neck should be trimmed from just below the base of the ear, and under the throat. Continue down the chest to just above the breast bone, round the side of the neck and over the shoulder. Begin to reduce your trimming of this area, just above the joint where the humerus meets the top and side of the upper front leg bone. There is a slight indentation here, so if you continue over this point, you will emphasise this characteristic. The natural lay of the hair is downwards, so allow the hair to grow longer here and over this joint.

As with the other parts of the Westie coat, the forelegs should also be hand-stripped, so that you have short, hard hair, as called for in the Breed Standard. This can be done on a weekly basis, but only a little at a time.

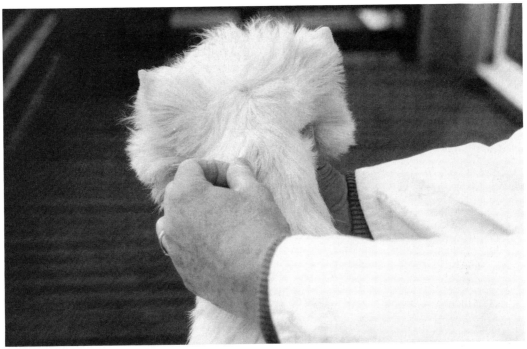

Start to trim from the back of the ears and down the back.

Continue stripping down the back.

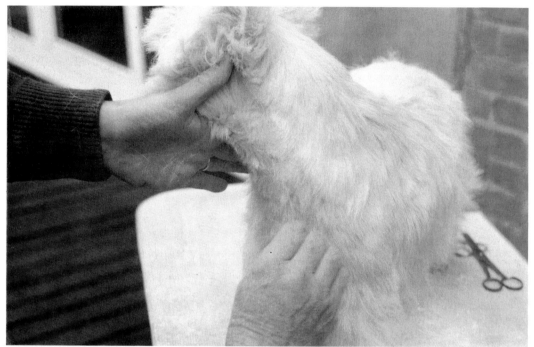

Hand stripping down the neck.

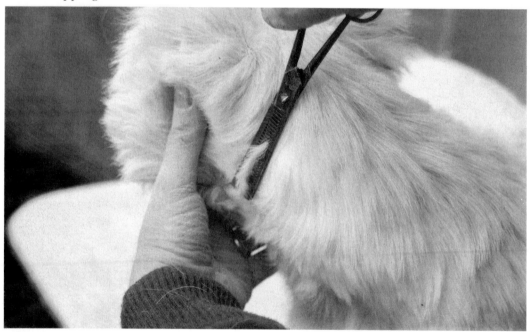

Blending from longer hair on neck and into shorter hair on underside of neck using thinning scissors.

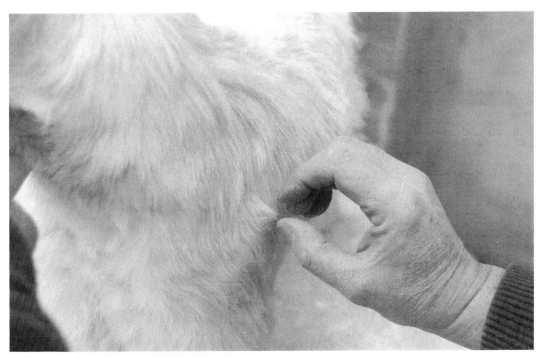

Stripping the shoulder.

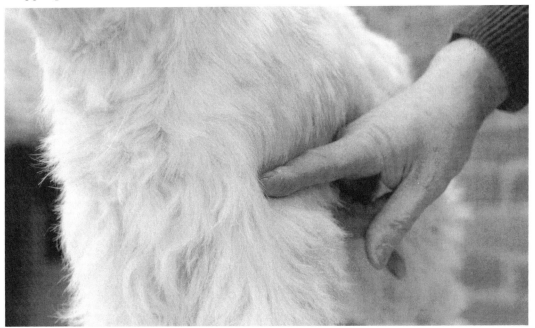

The point where the humerus meets the ulna: do not trim too severely at this point. Leave hair above a little longer.

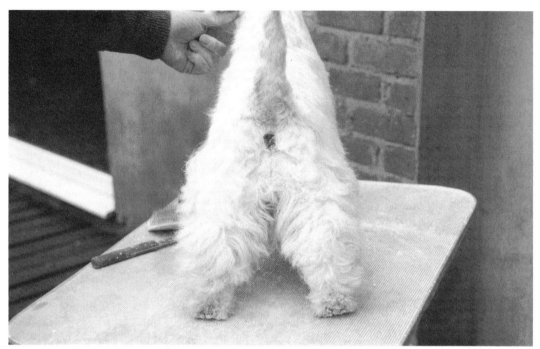

The rear brushed, but before trimming.

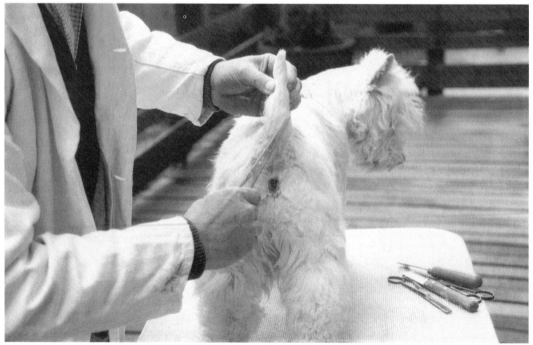

Trimming the back of the tail with scissors.

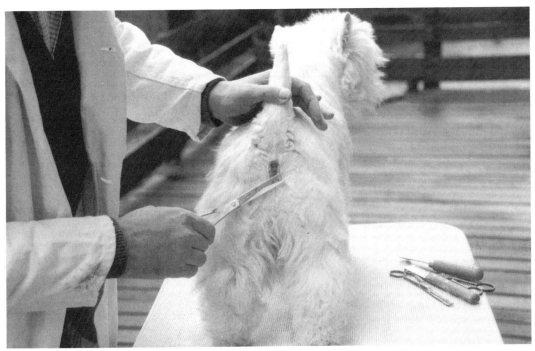

Trimming around the anus.

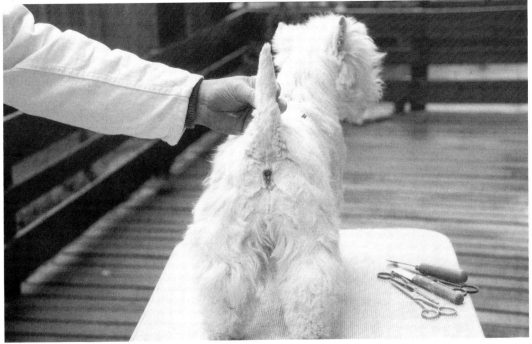

Right rear leg after trimming, compared with the rear left leg which is untrimmed.

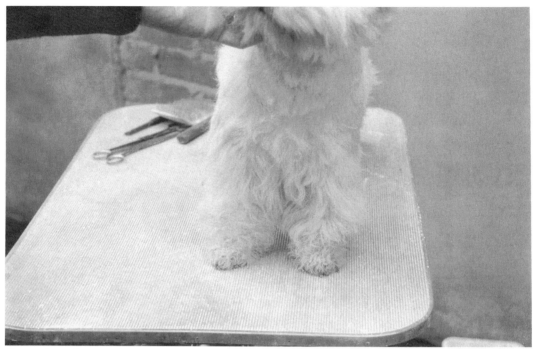

Front legs brushed, but untrimmed.

Leg and head furnishings are much slower growing, therefore it should be a very gradual process. The best way in which to do this is to back-comb the legs with your brush and pull the long hairs; the effect you should be trying to achieve is for all the hairs to be approximately the same length. If you allow the hair to grow without any stripping, you end up with a long silky coat on the legs, which will just blow around when the dog is on the move, possibly giving the judge the impression that the dog is moving incorrectly. When trimmed as explained, you will get that nice thick, dense coat, giving the legs that desirable tube-like effect. After filing the nails, cut the hair back to the nails and around the paw with your straight scissors, not forgetting to trim the hair between the pads, on the underside of the paw. The fine hair deep down between the pads should be checked each week; it is not unknown for this hair to start matting up, culminating in hard balls of fur, which can become very painful. Naturally, these balls of fur will have to be removed, otherwise your dog will eventually become lame.

The Westie must have a level back or level topline, as it is more commonly known, and the sides of the body should appear flattish, or slab-sided. Hair on the back should be shorter, but gradually gaining in length as you go down the sides and into the skirt. I have observed many people leaving the skirt to grow and grow, so much so, that it is almost touching the floor. Then they trim the bottom of the skirt,

First file the nails.

Trim round the paws up to the nails.

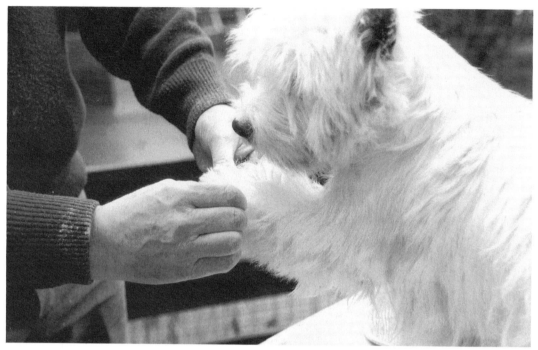

Hand strip some of the longer hairs.

using straight scissors, so that it hangs like a curtain. At the risk of repeating myself, I must emphasise that, as with the rest of the dog, the skirt should be hand-stripped in order to maintain a strong coat. If trimming is neglected, you will end up with a long, silky skirt, which will swing from side to side when the dog is on the move, or it will go in all directions when the dog shakes. If you feel the lower part is looking uneven, then tidy it up, but make sure you use thinning scissors rather than straight scissors, for you do not want a sharp line. The true art of trimming is in making it look natural, just as if that is the way the coat is meant to grow.

Once again, it is all a question of blending, so be careful not to over-trim just behind the shoulder blades. This could give the impression that the dog is dipping behind the shoulders. Similarly, do not over-trim just in front of the tail, as this can make the dog look as if it has got a low-set tail, or, coupled with close trimming behind the shoulders, it could give the impression of a roached back. The tail itself should be hand-stripped, but it will need a little shaping with the scissors to get the correct carrot shape. Scissor the rear of the tail quite closely; you do not want any feathering in this region. Be careful when trimming the very tip of the tail because no hair grows right on the end; allow the hair near the end of the tail to grow a little longer on all sides, so that it comes together in a point.

Trim over the thighs and down the rear legs, remembering a Westie when viewed

The finished front.

After doing a little hand stripping, shape the head with thinning scissors.

from above should appear wedge-shaped, i.e. narrower over the shoulders than over the hindquarters. You will find it will not be necessary to trim as often down the legs, but I would suggest light trimming is required, again on a weekly basis. The length of coat on the stifle should not be left long and dangling; it should be thick, hard hair, which follows the shape of the stifle. The same applies to the hock, where all soft dead hair should be removed. Once again, trim with straight scissors around the paw, not forgetting to trim the hair between the pads.

The rear, or the bottom, should be carefully trimmed. This area is rather sensitive, as one would imagine, therefore do not do a lot of hand-trimming in this region. I take the hair in very close, using thinning and straight scissors. Once you see how the hair grows around the anus, you will appreciate how very important it is to keep it clear. If the hair is allowed to grow over the anus without trimming, you will realise how easy it would be for the dog to end up all matted with faeces. It does not take a great deal of imagination to grasp how uncomfortable this would be for the dog. Trim round this area, using straight scissors, and making sure the opening to the anus is absolutely clear.

The trimming of the ears and shaping of the head is always the last thing I do, because the size of the head has to be in balance with the rest of the dog. It is no good just cutting and shaping the head with scissors, for eventually you will find the head hair will start to flop down and have no body to it. In order to get that fullness

Eng. Span. Ch. Ashgate Sallachy shows a well trimmed head, ready for the show ring.

in the head furnishings, it is essential to hand-strip the head on a regular basis, taking out a little hair once a week. This will soon give you that nice chrysanthemum-type head. Before starting to shape the dog's head, I always trim the ears. The old stalwarts of the breed always maintained you should pluck the end of the ears. However, I find there is no harm done by trimming and shaping with straight scissors. Trim the tips of the ears for about 0.5ins (12mm), cutting the hair on both the back and the front of the ear quite closely. When you are doing this, lay the scissors flat against the ear and cut in the direction the hair grows, which is outwards from the ear. Then trim the edges on these tips, following the contour of the ear but being extra careful not to cut the ear itself – otherwise you will end up with blood everywhere. In my opinion, you can get a much neater and tidier result if you trim in this way. When you have done this, you should have nicely pointed ears, ready for blending in with the head furnishings. Do not trim too much in front of the eye: the eyes should appear small, deep set and piercing. If you trim more than is necessary, you will give the appearance of large, round eyes, and thus give your Westie a completely foreign expression.

When you have completed your trimming, it is a good idea to give your dog a complete cleaning. For the pet owner, this is the best time to bath your dog if it is looking a little dirty. I always recommend using a good medicated shampoo for this. Exhibitors have to be a little more careful with their cleaning methods. Too much bathing will take out the oils that are in the coat and soften it, making it unmanageable for the show ring. I would therefore suggest a complete clean with chalk after you have finished trimming, treating the dog as if you are getting it ready for a show. In this way you will see if there are any areas that require further work – you will be amazed how different your dog will look once it has been cleaned and had a good shake. There is one other point which should always be remembered: you should never be able to see skin through the coat on a correctly trimmed dog. I repeat, *never!*

Once you have got your dog's coat in the show condition that you have been aiming for, make sure you keep it that way. As I keep on emphasising, if you trim a little each day, you will find it takes very little effort to keep your dog in prime coat. Even when a dog shakes, its coat should just fall into place, with very little further brushing being required. For those who have used, or still do use, hair lacquer, it will soon be a thing of the past if you spend the time and effort trimming, as I have described.

Chapter Nine

THE SHOW RING

If we assume that you have kept up with trimming your Westie on a regular basis, it should not be too difficult for you to do the final cleaning up and preparation in readiness for the show. Before going any further, I would mention that any dog which I am showing is not treated any differently from the rest of the kennel dogs. It is allowed to run and play with all the others, it gets just as filthy, and more importantly, it is allowed to enjoy itself. I never box or cage my dogs in order to keep them clean and ready for the next show. It is just as important to keep your dogs fit, with muscles well-toned, and in a generally healthy condition. There is no way this can be achieved by keeping dogs restricted in cages for hours on end; they have to be free-running.

However, there is a moment of reckoning, and you must have a cleaning-up routine in order to get your dog sparkling white, and looking good for the big day. The first requirement is an inexpensive hand-spray; the type used for house plants is ideal. This should be filled with a solution of approximately one-third dog shampoo to two-thirds water. Get your dog on the grooming table, facing towards you, and spray from the back of the head, down the neck, along the back and underneath the body, rubbing the solution well into the coat. If you over-do the spraying, and the dog becomes too wet, towel off the excess water so that the coat is just damp. Then, using your pin brush, start brushing loose chalk into the coat, again starting from behind the head and working down the neck, into the body and up to the tail. Turn the dog side on to you, and start brushing chalk into the underneath of the skirt, repeating this on the reverse side of the dog. Next, turn the dog facing away from you, so that you are able to repeat the same process on the rear, and on each hind leg. Now, have the dog facing you, so that you can do the same to the underside of the neck, the chest and the front legs. The head is the last part of the dog that I clean. The process is exactly the same: lightly spray the head, making sure you cover the eyes with thumb and first finger, apply the chalk in the same manner, again ensuring chalk does not get into the eyes. You will appreciate this is best done in an area outside the house, maybe in a garden shed or in the garage, but, wherever the dog is, it will need a good shake to get rid of the excess chalk. Then you can give the dog a good brush-down to remove the remaining chalk. The purpose of applying chalk is as a cleaning agent, and as such, it acts as a dry shampoo. You will find this method brings out all the dirt, without damaging the coat. Contrary to common belief, chalk will not whiten a coat, it only cleans it. If you are unfortunate enough to have a dog with a brown streak running down its back, which some Westies are prone to, no amount of chalk will make it white. In fact, it has the reverse effect and makes the brown stand out. The mouth is another area where brown staining may occur, and sometimes on the paws if your dog is prone to licking its feet. Staining is mainly caused by acid in the saliva, and it is a problem that you find with most Westies. I find the best way of reducing the staining is to give the dog a tablespoonful of Milk of Magnesia for two successive days, and then repeat the dose in a couple of weeks, if necessary.

In order to get your exhibit looking its best, this cleaning procedure should be carried out at least three times prior to the show. For example, if you are going to a show on a Saturday, then cleaning should begin on the Monday leading up to the show, and be repeated on the Wednesday, and again last thing on the Friday. When you arrive at the show, very little preparation is required before your class is called. The dog will just need a good brushing to liven up its coat after the journey. As for any further trimming, this should most definitely not be necessary. In my early years of showing, I can recall standing with my dog on the grooming table, trimming away, showing all and sundry how clever I was, and what a wonderful job I was doing. Then I heard a voice from the right of me saying: "That should have been done at home, laddie, before you came to the show. All you are doing is creating a mess!" That was the late Wyn Bertram of the Highstile kennel. It certainly brought me down to size and made me think. He was absolutely correct in what he said, even though I felt embarrassed at the time, and my pride had been hurt. It was one of the first constructive lessons I had, and later it was much appreciated. I have never forgotten this remark, and I always try to keep his lesson in mind. The more you think about it, the more sense it makes. At home you have all the time in the world to make the trimming look good, without any pressures. At the show you are limited to the time before you go into the ring, coupled to the fact your adrenalin will be pumping away – hardly the ideal conditions for making the best of your dog – but perfect for making an absolute hash of it!

When I am going to a show, I like to be there in good time. There is nothing worse than being late – you become nervous and up-tight, rushing around trying to get your dog ready. It is highly unlikely that, after all this, your dog will behave impeccably, showing itself beautifully, without putting a foot wrong. Unfortunately, feelings transmit down the leash, and your dog will be swift to sense your mood, whether it is good or bad. So if you get yourself into a harassed state, do not be surprised if your world-beater fails to perform when you finally get in the show ring. Give yourself plenty of time to get things sorted out and find where everything is located. Have a coffee, and both you and your dog can unwind after the journey. It is your responsibility to have the dog ready for its class, so keep on checking what stage the judging has reached.

If you are an absolute beginner, it is a good idea to go along to a show in order to learn about the general routine, before you actually enter your dog for competition. The whole business can be a lot more complicated than you would imagine. At a major Championship Show there are many classes for both dogs and bitches, and your entry will be determined by the age of your dog and any previous wins it has had. There is no point in entering a six-month-old puppy in every class available: you would be completely out of your depth in the higher classes and your entry fee will be wasted. It is far better to watch how experienced exhibitors handle their dogs in the ring, look at how they should stand, and how the dogs are moved when they are being judged. Then you can practise these techniques with your dog at home, so you are better prepared when you enter your first show. Some canine societies run puppy training classes on a one night a week basis, teaching you and your dog the craft of exhibiting. This helps to build up the confidence of both dog and exhibitor, which is a very important aspect of successful showing. Try not to be self-conscious: remember the judge and the ringside spectators are looking at the dog, not at you. However, it is important that you look clean and well-dressed; there is no use in having the dog looking immaculate, and for you to look a mess. You and your dog are working as a team, and you must complement each other. This is equally true for the novice as for the experienced exhibitor – surely it is worth the extra effort of making yourself look smart, especially after all the time you spent preparing your

Derek handling Ch. Olac Moonpoppy in the show ring.

Dave Freeman.

dog. The whole purpose of exhibiting is for the judge to compare each animal against the Breed Standard, and then against its contemporaries in each class. The general procedure of handling your dog when entering the ring is fairly straightforward, but you should remember to concentrate on your dog at all times to ensure that you are getting the best out of it. As you enter the ring all the dogs will be asked to stand in a line so the judge can make his first assessment. The judge may then ask all the dogs and handlers to walk round the ring in a circle, giving the judge the opportunity to compare movement in all the dogs. Each dog will be examined on the judge's table, where the mouth, eye, skull, coat and general conformation will be checked. You will then be requested to walk your dog, firstly in a triangle, then in a straight line. Try not to move too fast; you do not have to run or trot, just walk at a nice, steady pace. The reason for this is so that the judge is able to assess the front and rear movement, along with the overall carriage of the dog. Temperament is also assessed at this stage. No matter how good your dog may be in construction, it is no good if it has to be dragged, or walks round on its belly, with its tail tucked underneath its legs. When these assessments have been made, the judge will select the five dogs which he or she considers best, and place them from first to fifth. When all the classes have been judged, the ring steward will then request, on behalf of the judge, all unbeaten dogs to come back into the ring, so that each winning dog will be challenging the others for which the judge considers to be the best dog. At a Championship Show in the UK, this dog would then be presented with the Challenge Certificate award. The whole exercise is then repeated with the bitches, so that you are left with the best male and the best female, which challenge for Best of Breed. If a dog or bitch is to gain its Championship title, it must receive a total of three Challenge Certificates under three separate judges. This may not sound a lot to the layman, but I can assure you it is not easy, especially when you consider that the average breed entry for a Championship Show is anything from ninety to one hundred and fifty dogs.

In the United States dogs are judged on a points basis, and a dog must win a total of fifteen points in order to become a Champion. The number of points a dog gets is dependent on the number of dogs it beats, rather than the number of dogs entered, and varies depending on show location. The total of fifteen points must include two 'majors', which are three, four or five point wins.

Chapter Ten

JUDGING THE BREED

As a judge, I have frequently been asked how do I choose one dog from another, particularly when there are so many dogs in a class. To the untrained eye, it must appear very confusing, especially in a breed such as the West Highland White Terrier when all the dogs are white and look more or less the same size. The Breed Standard (analysed and interpreted in Chapter Three) is the result of many years study of the breed in question by those most closely associated with it. The official version is compiled by the national Kennel Club in conjunction with the breed clubs, and its aim is to protect the breed and maintain its type. Listed below is the scale of points which should be awarded by the judge when he or she is assessing a dog against the Breed Standard, and against its fellow competitors. Hopefully, this will help to enlighten the uninitiated over the mystery of judging, but it must be remembered that each judge may interpret the Breed Standard differently from the next. It is a very subjective business, although it must be stressed, once again, that every judge should always judge to the Breed Standard.

SCALE OF POINTS

General appearance and size.............................20 points
Coat and colour...10 points
Skull ....5 points

Eyes..5 points
Muzzle and teeth..15 points
Ears...5 points
Neck...5 points
Body...10 points
Legs and feet...10 points
Tail..5 points
Movement..10 points

Before anyone decides to embark on a judging career, I firmly believe that you need a proper grounding in the breed, with a proven track record, before accepting any judging assignments. All too often I have seen people allocated to judge our breed for one show or another, after a very brief show career. They have had very little chance to learn much about dogs, let alone the breed. Even worse, I have also seen these people put their names down for judging other breeds, which I find most frightening. I believe it shows a lack of responsibility for the job in hand. Remember, people are spending a lot of time preparing their dogs, and they are paying good money, not only in entry fees, but also to travel to the show; therefore, they do have the right to a competent judge, rather than somebody on an ego trip.

There is no way one can learn enough about dogs in a couple of years to justify accepting judging appointments, but you continually hear people complaining that they have not, as yet, been asked to judge. They go along to the shows, exhibit their dog, and when they have finished, they pack up and go home. Whereas the aspiring judge should use the opportunity to go to the various ringsides and watch other breeds being judged. This is the only way to learn about dogs in general, rather than confining your interest to your own breed. For years, Joan, my wife, and I have stood or sat watching all kinds of breeds in the show ring. In our early showing days these were mainly the terrier breeds, and we learned so much from many an old terrier man – some of the tales they could tell would make your hair stand on end! Sadly, there are not many of these people left, and, to this day, I value the time I spent with them. However, the important point is to broaden your interest when you are at a dog show and avoid the mistake of becoming tunnel-visioned, or you will stagnate and end up learning very little, or, at worst, nothing at all.

When you are watching proceedings at the ringside, observe how a judge goes over a dog, and then follows the dog when it is moving. If it is not moving correctly, or looks awkward when standing, try and assess, in your own mind, what is causing the problem. If you are unable to evaluate this, or any other problem, do not be

*Derek in intense
concentration
judging a class.*

afraid to ask anybody with more experience. Most people will be only too pleased to help, and to share their knowledge. However, do not interrupt somebody who is getting their dog ready to go into the ring; they will be far too busy and preoccupied to deal with your enquiry. There are times when I must appear very rude – when people speak to me and receive a brusque answer, or worse, no answer at all. This is never intentional, and I apologise to anyone I appear to have ignored. It is simply that the adrenalin is flowing, and I am deep in concentration. After I have finished showing, I am more than happy to give the novice as much time and as much help as they require – and I am sure this goes for any other experienced exhibitor.

Learn to be critical of your own stock. If you are unable to do this, how can you, in all honesty, judge other people's dogs in a fair, unbiased manner? This is fundamental to being a successful judge, and every exhibitor has the right to expect a judge to assess dogs without any preconceptions or prejudice. Equally, if you are unable to see the faults in your own animals, how can you ever hope to improve your own lines? After all, producing improved stock is the whole object of breeding and exhibiting in the show ring. I have heard some people extolling the so-called virtues of their dog, attempting to brainwash others into believing it is far better than it really is. At the same time, they will mention a string of successful dogs and invent faults in them. Try not to be taken in by these unsporting competitors. Take a long, hard look at the dog they are boasting about, and form your own opinion. A truly good dog does not need to be shouted about – the quality stands out a mile.

There is one way that you, an aspiring judge, can improve your knowledge and appreciation of the breed, and that is by asking the owner of a top-quality animal if you can go over the dog yourself. You will be amazed how much you can learn from this exercise; it will help you to learn what you should be looking for, and it is an experience that will stand you in very good stead in the show ring. The West Highland White Terrier has a profuse coat, and so it is very easy to be fooled into drawing the wrong conclusions when you look at a dog, as opposed to actually going over it. It has been proved, time after time, how important it is to have your hands on a dog, before deciding on its faults or merits. I have lost count of the number of times when I have read a judge's report, which stated how much better a certain dog was to go over than they had first imagined.

Once you have served your apprenticeship, and, believe me, it is a true apprenticeship and should last approximately some seven years, you may get the chance to judge one or two minor or Limit shows. These sort of shows are ideal for getting the novice judge started, and they are good groundwork for the future. Do not try to run before you can walk by judging at a higher level too quickly; you could very soon find yourself in at the deep end and out of your depth. When you start judging there are a few rules that you should try to follow; in fact, they are worth observing no matter what level you are judging at.

1. Always dress smartly and look the part.
2. Give each dog the same time and judgment, even if there is one which is obviously a pet and untrained for the show ring. Remember each exhibitor has paid exactly the same amount of money to enter their dog, and they expect, and deserve, the same consideration as any other dog in the show ring.
3. Be courteous to the exhibitor at all times; they are giving you the privilege of going over their dog.
4. Never try holding a conversation with the exhibitor in the show ring.
5. Never hold a conversation with people outside the ring while you are judging; this gives exhibitors the impression that you are not interested in their dogs.
6. Do not talk to the exhibitor about their dog while you are in the show ring. In fact, I would suggest that it is bad policy to make any comment about anybody's dog at any time, unless the owner specifically requests your opinion.

Some of these points may seem obvious, but you would be surprised how many judges make one, or even all, of these mistakes at one time or another. It is so easy to fall into the trap without thinking, and invariably, it gives the wrong impression.

Assessing movement in a dog is one of the most important aspects of judging. If an animal cannot move correctly, it is incapable of doing the job of work it was bred for. Movement starts from the front, with well laid shoulders, which allows the dog to have the correct length of stride, with good pace on the move. Quick, short steps do not constitute good movement. Similarly, the construction of the hindquarters is most important; this is the engine-room, the powerhouse of a dog. A good bend of stifle, coupled with short hocks and well-muscled thighs, gives the Westie the drive and ability to cover the ground with a non-stilted movement. The correct movement in a Westie can be likened to that of an old steam engine, when the piston rods move the main driving wheels with power and smoothness of action.

The size of the Westie has to be carefully monitored, otherwise we will be straying from the Breed Standard, and this is just as important as any other fault in the breed. Obviously, you cannot expect every dog to be 'spot on' the size that is stipulated. In the English Breed Standard this is 28 cms (11 ins) to the withers; the American Standard asks for males to be 11 ins and bitches to be 10 ins. However, I would suggest the maximum deviation should be no more than half an inch on either side of the stipulated size.

The Westie has a very distinctive head, and this can present problems when trying to breed to the requirements of the Breed Standard. A head that is too long and narrow in the foreface gives a foxy appearance. This is fine for a fox, but it looks horrible on a Westie. A typical Westie should have a broad muzzle: a useful guideline is to aim for a slightly shorter distance from nose to stop than from stop to occiput. The skull should be broad, slightly domed, and with thick protruding eyebrows to protect the eyes. The eyes should be almond-shaped and as dark as possible. The cheeks should be filled in under the eyes, a dished out appearance under the eye and overshot or undershot teeth are most undesirable.

When you are judging, especially at Championship level, you should always bear in mind that your job is to send the best exhibit on the day to be assessed in the Terrier Group. The dog must not only be the best dog, but it must also look the part: it must have the style and presence to compete against the Best of each Terrier breed. Hopefully, your Best of Breed will then be chosen as Best Terrier, and will compete for the ultimate honour of Best in Show. Always remember that the dog you choose is not only the representative of the breed, but is also a reflection of you as a judge.

Chapter Eleven

PERSONAL EXPERIENCES

When I think back to my first venture into the world of dog showing, it makes me realise just how much things have changed in our sport over the years. Our first outing was to a Match Meeting. These were invariably held midweek in large smoke-filled rooms over public houses, where the landlords agreed to allow these events to take place. I suppose they worked on the theory that if the place was full, they would sell more beer and spirits. The more I recall these times, the more they appear like holograms of the distant past, for this is how dog showing first began in the early 1900s. These Matches were great for not only meeting people, but also being introduced to the different breeds of dogs. It was always fascinating to listen to all the chatter about dogs and dog shows (in between the clinking of glasses and a few dog barks): "Did you go to last week's ... we were robbed!" "What did you think of the judge? All we got was a reserve, and a very highly commended (VHC). He was rubbish!" "Oh, we had two firsts, and Best in Show there, we thought he was quite a good judge, really ...".

Unfortunately, these sort of events do not take place today in the same kind of atmosphere, and I think people starting in dog showing today, or in the more recent past, are missing out on an awful lot of fun, and a very useful learning ground – for this was the grass roots of dog showing. There was many a Sanction show in the evenings during the working week. You would rush home to have a quick bite to eat, give the dog a hasty spit and polish, and off you would go! If you were lucky, you would arrive home at maybe 10 to 10.30pm, a little tired, with a couple of small rosettes pinned to the chest, but feeling as proud as Punch. These shows were also a very good training ground for aspiring judges; you were never sure what breeds would come along, so you had the opportunity of handling all shapes and sizes.

After progressing through all the Match Meetings, Sanction, Limit and Open Shows, it was finally time to try my luck at my first really big event – a Championship show. Full of nerves and trepidation, I entered for the Manchester show, which was in the area where I live. It was quite obvious from the moment we arrived that I had entered a different league. For a start, there were a lot more dogs of the same breed entered, and the overall standard, both in quality of dogs and presentation, was that much higher. I soon learned a lot about professionalism in handling. If anybody was responsible for giving me the drive and determination to keep going after my first Championship shows, it was the professional handler Fred Sills, albeit unknowingly. In those days, if Fred was in your class you could guarantee he would always be placed first, and invariably he would be in my class. I can still remember talking to Joan on a return journey from a show, and saying: "One day I am going to beat that man, just you see; one day I will beat him." In reality, I was trying to convince myself as much as anyone else! There was one little trick of Fred's which I soon discovered, and I was determined to counteract it. When all the dogs in the class had been seen by the judge, we would all line up waiting for final assessment and for the placings to be made. Fred would always stand his dog approximately two feet further out of line, and nearer the judge. The result was that the judge's eye would always keep going to his dog, because it seemed to be standing alone – and each and every time, Fred would come first! Twelve months later, and again at the Manchester Championship Show, Fred did his old trick, so I moved my dog out with him. Fred responded by moving his dog out again, and I immediately followed suit. However, unnoticed by us, each exhibitor was doing the same thing, and before we realised it we had all advanced halfway across the ring. You can imagine the judge's face, it was a real howler! Anyway, we were all asked to move further back, and that was the end of that little trick. Fred is one of those characters (of which there are so few these days) who is a really likable rogue who would do anybody a favour, rather than do them harm.

Feeding dogs is one of the key issues when you start breeding and showing dogs, and these days it has become a very competitive area with so many manufacturers hunting for business. Obviously, every breeder makes his own choice, but when you start becoming successful in the show ring, it is not long before you become sought after by the sales reps. I remember my first encounter with a very well known, and possibly the largest, dog food manufacturer in the UK. It happened at the West of England Championship Show, which is held at Malvern, a most delightful area. My dog, Moonraker, had just been awarded the CC, and we were waiting for the challenge for the Best of Breed. Three men approached me, complete with cine camera, enquiring if my dogs were fed this famous brand of tinned meat. At that time I did not use this food, and I told them so. They replied: "That's a shame, because we wanted to use you in our advertisement campaign." With tongue in cheek and a smile on my face, I quickly replied: "If the money is right they will eat anything!" To be fair, they did say they could not do this, as the dogs had to be genuinely reared on their food. From our first Champion, Moonraker, we bred our first big winner – a bitch called Ch. Olac Moonbeam, who was a real lady. In 1975 she was the first Westie ever to qualify in a heat at the SKC (Scottish Kennel Club) Show for the finals of the all breeds Pup Of The Year competition. The judge was the late Mrs Judy De Cassembroot. Moonbeam was the top winning bitch in 1976 with eight CCs, Reserve in the Terrier Group at the Southern Counties Show, followed by winning the Terrier Group and Reserve Best in Show at Blackpool. This was followed up with her also winning the Terrier Group at Border Union. It was while I was showing Moonbeam in Scotland that I was approached once more by the very same group of cameramen from the dog food company. On this occasion they inquired if I would be willing to undergo a short test-run on film, explaining in my own words what I thought were the advantages in using their product. Having sampled a couple of glasses of that fine liquid sustenance which Scotland is famed for, I agreed, even though I was none the wiser about their product. The camera started rolling, and the producer said to me: "Now then, Mr Tattersall, in your own words, what is it about our tinned meat that appeals to you?" Making sure my hair was in place, and turning to give my best profile, I replied: "It is so convenient and easy to use, just open the can and pour the contents out." For a split second there was silence, and then I realised I had not said quite the right thing, for suddenly there was giggling coming from Joan, who was standing behind me, and there was a worried look on the face of the producer. "What do you mean – 'it pours out'? Do you mean the jelly?" he asked. Realising I had made a big blunder, I quickly replied with an authoritative voice; "Why yes, of course!" It was obvious that I had never used a can of their meat, because, as I was later to learn, it is solid in its consistency. In fact, they had the last laugh, because I later became a great convert to their product, and I have used it for years!

Ch. Olac Moondream (UK Nord. Ch. Tweed Tartan Caledonia – Ch. Olac Moonbeam) and Ch. Olac Moondrift (Ch. Backmuir Noble James – Miranda Moon

Joan Tattersall and Barbara Woodhouse after Ch. Halfmoon Of Olac won the Pup of the Year contest in 1980.

Of Olac) were the next two dogs from my kennels to make an impression in the show ring. In 1979 Moondrift was the top Westie with ten CCs, and four Reserve CCs. It was with these two Westies that I won the double at Leeds Championship Show, taking both the dog CC and the bitch CC on the same day, under the same judge, Mrs Heather Davies. After a lot of persuasion I eventually agreed to let Moondrift go to America, where he gained his American and Canadian titles. At the time I had no bitches which I could use him on, so I gave way and let him go. Although I was delighted with his success in America, as far as my kennel was concerned it proved to be the biggest mistake I ever made, because within eighteen months I did have bitches which would have been ideal for him.

Ch. Halfmoon of Olac (Emma) took honours in the Pup of the Year in 1980, and the final was staged at London Zoo. After Emma had been given the overall winner by Mrs Pam Cross-Stern, the Press photographers wanted a photograph of Joan holding Emma, and they wanted to include the famous dog trainer, the late Barbara Woodhouse. The idea was to have Emma face to face with Barbara, but try as she may, there was no way Barbara could get Emma to look at her. All the years of honing her skills in training dogs could not help Barbara on this occasion! Our next Champion was Ch. Olac Moonpoppy (Olac Mooncopy At Marank – Ch. Halfmoon Of Olac). 'Tilly', as she was called, not only won Best Puppy in Show at the East of England show, but she went on to win six CCs with one Reserve Best Terrier at Midland Counties, and one Best Terrier at the Welsh Kennel Club at Builth Wells. We managed to qualify another of our dogs for the Pup of the Year finals in 1985, with Olac Moonmaverick. Although he did not win the final, he has more than made up for it by being the sire of Ch. Olac Moonpilot (Paddy).

I have already given most of the details of Paddy's wins, but there is one question that people always ask me: "How did it feel to win the big one – Crufts?" In fact, it all started twelve months earlier, when the majority of exhibitors thought we were going to win Crufts in February 1989. They based their assumptions on the fact that Paddy had been the top winning dog all breeds for the whole of 1988; therefore, in their eyes it stood to reason that we would pull it off at the next Crufts. However, I had been telling people it was very rare for the top dog to win the big one. I don't know why this should be so, but time and time again it has proved to be the case. That year we had decided to travel on a specially booked coach for Crufts, leaving home at approximately 2.00am and travelling to London. In the event, we were awarded Best of Breed under Mr Wyn Bertram (Highstile), but we failed to impress our Terrier Group judge, and were not even pulled out for the final cut. Feeling a little tired and disappointed, we climbed aboard the coach for our return journey, to be greeted with lots of commiserations from our travelling companions. When we arrived home, the first thing we did after tending to Paddy, was to relax and have a nice cup of tea before going to bed. We decided to watch the news on television, and the first thing to appear was an item on the famine in Ethiopia. It showed small children, with even smaller tin cans, walking two miles to get water, whereas we had just walked into our kitchen and filled a kettle for a cup of tea. I hate to count the number of times we do this in a day. With this I turned to Joan, saying: "That puts everything in perspective. What does it matter that we have been beaten at a dog show? Our dogs eat better than they do, and in comparison to those poor people we are kings." Don't get me wrong – I still like to win; but this put a whole new light on

Derek and Joan at home with 'Paddy'.   *Marc Henrie.*

what we were doing. When all is said and done, this is our hobby, and we are lucky to be able to pursue it, when some poor wretches can only worry about where the next meal is coming from. I am sure most people in the dog world will sympathise with what I am saying.

When I eventually won Crufts, the following year, there was one moment which stands out in my mind. On this occasion, Joan and I decided that rather than travel on a coach as we had done the previous year, we would book a room along with friends in a small hotel just round the corner from Earls Court, the show venue. We had a nice leisurely drive down to London on the Friday, and this gave me and the dog time to relax in time for the show on the following day. Saturday turned out to be quite a day, for we won the breed, under breed specialist Mrs Rosemary Pritchard (Mellwyn), and proceeded to win the Terrier Group, judged by Vincent Mitchell. That night we had a small celebration with our friends by going out and having a nice Italian meal, with a bottle of wine. The following day we did not have to be at the show until the afternoon, which was just as well, since I had agreed for somebody to come to the hotel that morning in order for them to use Paddy at stud. Our room was so small you could just squeeze round each side of the double bed, therefore there was only one place we could carry out the mating of these two dogs, and that was on the bed. I often wonder if Paddy tells all his doggie friends that after you win the Group at Crufts, part of the prize seems to be you get a bitch on a double bed in a hotel! The afternoon seemed very long, and all sorts of things were going through my mind. Paddy, however, was oblivious to it all, lying fast asleep on his grooming table. At last, the time drew near for the challenge of Best in Show. I woke up Paddy, started brushing him so he would be ready in time for the big occasion. All of a sudden there seemed to be a lot of activity, with stewards arranging people in the order they were to enter the ring. Almost before I knew it, four of the finalists were being called to the arena, and there we were standing on that famous green baize carpet, in readiness for our grand entrance. It was at this point that I realised how big the arena really is. I know I had been in the very same ring the previous day, but then there were more dogs and people in the ring. However, once I had entered and we were on the move, we just concentrated and got down to the job in hand. After each dog had been inspected and had its turn in being moved and posed, the moment of truth finally arrived. While I could see the judge, Mrs Sommerfield, out of the corner of my eye, moving in my direction, I felt I could not look up in case she was going to one of the other dogs either side of me. However, I did hear the crowds starting to shout: "It's the Westie!" I did not look up until Mrs Sommerfield was about two metres away from me, with her hand held out to shake my hand. This is that moment that every exhibitor hopes to experience; it is the pinnacle in your show career, the culmination – all those patient years of hard work and planning suddenly coming to fruition. My mind was in a complete whirl. As Crufts winner, the following twelve months were hectic, with both Paddy and myself in demand for charity work, and consequently we met many very nice people. We totalled approximately 14,000 miles travelling up and down the country to one charity event after another. I felt we could not ask for expenses as they were all trying to raise money for charity, so it proved quite an expensive year, but I thoroughly enjoyed it and would do it all again.

Obviously, I am delighted with the success I have experienced with my dogs in the years that we have been part of this sport, and naturally, I hope it may continue. However, I must admit that these days I get just as big a thrill from judging, not only my own breed, but other breeds as well. Over the years I have always shown an interest in other breeds; I have owned German Shepherds, an American Cocker Spaniel, Scottish Terriers, and a Miniature Schnauzer, and I consider myself to be a true dog man, rather than a one-breed fancier.

Chapter Twelve

WESTIES IN AMERICA

In 1908, for one year only, the West Highland White Terrier was first listed in the records of the American Kennel Club by the name 'Roseneath Terrier'. This was the name given to the dogs owned by the Duke of Argyll in the very early days of the breed in the UK. On May 31st 1909 this was changed, and in that year fourteen dogs and ten bitches were registered as West Highland White Terriers with the American Kennel Club. Among them was Cream Of The Skies (Ossian – Sky Lady), a two-year-old import, owned by R. D. Humphrey and Philip Boyer of Mt. Kisco, New York, who became the breed's first Champion in that year. By 1986 the number of Champions was one hundred and seventy, and the number of registrations had risen to 8,635.

Because of the sheer size of the North American continent, the show scene is run very much on its own lines. The distance between show sites is so vast that many breeders put their dogs with professional handlers in order for them to be exhibited on the show circuit. An indication of the size of these circuits is that many handlers can be away from home for as long as five or six weeks, just travelling from show to show. Obviously, the majority of people cannot be away from their homes or businesses for such an extended period, particularly when they have other dogs to look after. I have always said that the show scene in the UK is like a travelling circus, but the American scene is even more like one, with the tremendous organisation and management that is needed to set up a show, with all the thousands of exhibitors and the vast range of trade stalls, and then moving on to the next location, all in a matter of days. One of the drawbacks of the system is the expense involved in employing a professional handler, and therefore it is not uncommon for a dog to be shown just as long as is necessary to gain its Champion title, and then to retire from the ring. Alternatively, if the dog proves to be a real quality animal, winning with style and maybe doing well in Groups or the Best in Show ring, the owner may consider "specializing" the dog. That means keeping the dog with a professional handler and campaigning it on a regular basis. If it gets to this stage, the owner may try and set up a syndicate of people who are willing to buy a share in the dog, thus spreading the expenses. This keeps the dog on the campaign trail, and offsets the high costs involved.

The fortunes of the Westie in the United States are watched over by the Westie Club of America. Established in 1909, the WHWTCA has hundreds of members all over the United States, Canada, and many other countries including the United Kingdom. The Club's primary responsibilities include formulating the Breed Standard, maintaining programmes for all interested persons and holding national Specialties. On a more local level, regional clubs cater for the more immediate needs of Westie fanciers in their repective areas. Some of these functions are breeders' referrals, handling and grooming classes, educational and social functions, holding local Specialty shows and generally projecting a positive image for the breed.

With the exception of the Annual National Montgomery or Specialty (Club) shows, it would be fair to say that dog shows in America are considerably smaller than those in the UK. A few years ago I had the privilege of judging Westies at the Sacramento Kennel Club show. The number of Westies entered was sixty-nine, which was considered to be an excellent entry. The total entry of all breeds was approximately 3,000 dogs, which compares with the average entry of 10,000 at a British show. The following weekend I visited another Northern Californian all-breed show, where there were fifteen Westies entered, which is the average for an American Championship show. The exception is the Westminster show, which is the equivalent of Crufts, and this has all the razzamatazz and showmanship to be associated with the dog world's premier event. Westminster usually draws an entry of approximately 2,500 dogs, to be compared with over 20,000 entries at Crufts in 1992.

In the UK breeders have no problem in taking their bitches to any stud dog of their choice because distances are relatively small. In America, a breeder may have to ship their bitch by air, in order to use the stud dog of their choice. Again, this adds

Am. Ch. Olac Mooncloud imported by Rita and Bob Widden.

enormously to the overall cost of breeding a litter. However, this has not detracted from the popularity of dog showing, and Westies have enjoyed a good deal of support in the show world in recent years. Many of the top winning Westies have been imported from the UK – the breed's country of origin. In the early seventies the Rev. Michael Collings of the Purston kennel (the same Michael Collings who now has a great deal of success with Welsh Terriers) exported Ch. Purston Pinmoney Pedlar (Ch. Pillerton Peterman – Pinmoney Pride) to Mrs B. G. Frame. This dog created quite an impression on the show scene and went on to win fifty Best in Show awards, stretching from 1970 to 1974. I believe, to this day, he is still the top Best in Show winner in the history of the breed in America. Over the decade of the seventies, it is amazing how many times Ch. Pillerton Peterman's name kept appearing on pedigrees.

In 1972 Mrs C. Jones imported Ch. Pillerton Peterkin (Ch. Pillerton Peterman – Pillerton Polka) and Ch. Pinmoney Puck (Ch. Pillerton Peterman – Trudy's Delight), owned jointly by Mrs Keenan and Mrs Schiele, and both of these dogs went on to win Best in Show awards. In fact, Pinmoney Puck won a total of nine Best in Shows. Another of the Peterman offspring, this time a bitch, Ch. Purston Polly Perkins (Ch. Pillerton Peterman – Birkfell Screech Owl) also went on to win the coveted Best in Show award. The Pillerton line was to have an influence on a lot of breeding lines, not only in the UK but also in America. In 1975 Mrs Sylvia Kearsey and her breeding stock, including Peterman, went to live in the United States, where she successfully joined her Pillerton kennel with the Biljonblue kennel belonging to William Ferrara and John Price. The old saying "One man's loss is another man's gain", was certainly true in this case. Sylvia returned to the UK in 1983, but, unfortunately, no longer takes such an active part in the breeding and showing of Westies. However, she still judges the breed at Championship shows, so she is still able to contribute her experience and wealth of knowledge to the breed. In 1974 Dr Hunt imported a dog, once again exported by Michael Collings. This was in the shape of Ch. Ardenrun Andsome Of Purston (Whitebriar Jonfair – Ardenrun Agitator), who went on to win twenty-eight Best in Shows. I am pleased to say I have played my small part on the American show scene, when Rita and Bob Widden imported Ch. Olac Mooncloud, sired by Eng. Ch. Olac Moonraker. This dog went on to be the top winning Westie in the United States in 1981. For two years running, 1983 and 1984, Ch. Pagan Ghost sired by Mooncloud and bred by Jim Sanders, won Best of Breed at the prestigious Westminster Show.

A dog which hit the headlines during the mid to late eighties is Ch. Mac-Ken-Char's Irish Navigator. This dog was bred and owned by Joanne and Jaimi Glodek. Not only has he been a consistent winner, but he is more than proving himself as a

Eng. Am. and Can. Ch. Olac Moondrift.   *MikRon*

prolific stud of quality pups, many of which have gone on, and still are going on, to gain their Champion status. Another dog hitting the high notes at present is Ch. Biljonblue's Best Of Times, owned by Robert and Susan Ernst of the Sweet Sounds kennel. He is a great great grandson of Ch. Pillerton Peterman, and, dare I say it, one can see a very strong resemblance. To date, he has already won seventeen Group Ones, also winning the Western Pennsylvania Specialty. The same kennel also boasts the multiple Best in Show winner Ch. Principal's MacGyver.

It is always gratifying to see stock that you have bred and exported doing well in their adopted country. Ch. Olac Moonpenny Of Bel-West, imported by Hal Heubal, was one such bitch. Her highest achievement was winning Best of Opposite Sex out of 114 bitches entered at the 1989 WHWTCA Specialty. Due to her accomplishments, the Bel-West kennel were the recipients of two annual Awards from the American Westie Club. One was for the bitch, who earned the most Best of Breed awards in 1988, the other was for the most Best of Opposite Sex wins in 1988. It was also especially pleasing for me to see Ch. Olac Moonshine (Ital. Ch. Arnholme Aces High – Eng. Ch. Olac Moonpoppy), a bitch that I exported to Alice Shepard, tie for Number One Westie dam in 1989, after having a very successful show career. Another dog from my kennel, Ch. Olac Moonwalker (Eng. Ch. Olac Moonpilot – Eng. Ch. Olac Moonpoppy) is currently doing extremely well for his owner, Mrs C. C. McClellan, and handlers Dee and Dick Hanna. I understand that he is lying third top Westie in America at the present time.

One or two dogs have been imported from Sweden during the eighties, and have made quite a name for themselves. The first of these was Ch. Glenncheck May Be. I knew this bitch quite well, for I gave her Best in Show when judging the Swedish Club Specialty, the year before she was exported to the United States. The next import was a dog bred by Birgitta Hasselgren, and owned by Gary Gabriel and Florence MacMillan. He became Nordic Am. Ch. Tweed Take By Storm or 'Oliver' (Int. Nord. Ch. Bushey's Major Storm – Tweed Thistle Leerose), and has proved to be another consistent winner with a lot of British breeding behind him. He completed his career with nineteen Best in Shows, along with numerous Specialty Bests and Group wins. When he arrived in America from Sweden, Oliver had already won thirteen CCs at approximately eighteen months of age. He was top winning Westie in 1988, and followed this up with being Number Two top Westie in 1989. To date, he has sired over twenty Champions. Int. Dan. Am. Ch. Bushey's Mr O'Smash (Swed. & World Ch. Smash I'm Sparkling – Swed. Ch. Bushey's Miss O'Malley) was another Swedish import to make an impression with his style and quality, and notched up a series of wins. 'Robin' was bred by Britta Roos-Borjeson, and is co-owned by Gary Gabriel and Florence MacMillan.

Ch. Mac-Ken-Char's Irish Navigator: the top producing Westie of all time with over 100 Champions.

Am. Ch. Mac-Ken-Char's Fantasy Blaze: an Irish Navigator grandson and a Specialty and Sweepstakes winner at seven months. He has produced five Champions to date.

Am. Ch. Mac-Ken-Char's White Shadow: another Irish Navigator grandson. He was second top winning Westie in 1990.

Ch. Biljonblue's Best Of Times: a great grandson of Ch. Pillerton Peterman – and bears a strong resemblance.

Nord. Am. Ch. Tweed Take By Storm: a consistent winner in the show ring.   Missy Yuhl.

Again, this dog has mainly British breeding behind him. He was Best of Winners at the prestigious Montgomery County Kennel Club show in 1989, and has been Best of Breed winner at numerous Specialty shows, including the Southeast Texas Specialty in August 1991. He is already proving his worth at stud, and has sired another winner in the shape of Ch. L'Esprit's Logan Of Mirage. This young dog, who gained his title in very quick time, is a grandson of Take By Storm. Another dog from the same kennel to make his mark is Ch. Waterford Of Wyndam, who won Best of Breed at the Westminster Kennel Club show in 1988. This is no mean feat, because there is always very stiff competition at this famous show.

Int. Am. Ch. Bushey's Mister O'Smash: a Swedish import who has made a big impression. *Missy Yuhl.*

Ch. L'Esprit's Logan Of Mirage: he gained his title in very quick time.   Missy Yuhl.

Am. Ch. Waterford Of Wyndam: Best of Breed at the Westminster Kennel Club Show in 1988.   *Missy Yuhl.*

Am. Ch. Kilkerran D'Artagnan: a multiple Best in Show winner.

Wayne and Kathy Kompare's Kilkerran Westies are causing quite a stir in the Westie world with a nice run of success. When I judged the Sacramento show, I gave Reserve Winners Dog to Kilkerran D'Artagnan, who finished with three Specialty wins from the Bred-by-Exhibitor class. He went on to be the Kompares' first multiple Best in Show winner, and not only was he a big winner in his own right, but he also sired the Kompares' latest Best in Show winner, Ch. Kilkerran Quintessence. This dog has won four Bests and two Specialty Bests in 1991. Although his show career has only just begun for his owner-handler, Nancy Spelke, he is already outshining two others of the Kompares' specials, Ch. Kilkerran N'Wicket A Kut Above and Ch. Gingerbread Kilkerran Katie. Dr James and Elizabeth Boso have seen their dog, Ch. Glenfinnan's Something Dandy (Eng. Am. Ch. Whitebriar Jeronimo – Am. Can. Ch. Craigty's Something Special), enjoy a successful show career, including winning Best of Breed at the Westminster Show in 1986, and now they are thrilled to see his stock doing a repeat performance. His son, Ch. Holyrood's Hootman O'Shely Bay, is a multiple Best in Show and Specialty winner with twelve Specialty Best in Shows. His grandson, Ch. Round Town Ivan The Terror, who is only two years of age, has already notched up six Best in Shows.

Am. Ch. Kilkerran Quintessence: a Best in Show winner, sired by Am. Ch. Kilkerran D'Artagnan.

Am. Ch. Kilkerran N'Wicket A Kut Above: Best in Show winner. *Missy Yuhl.*

Am. Ch. Glenfinnan's Something Dandy: now producing top-quality stock.

Something Dandy or 'Nicky', as he is affectionately called, is now nine years old and has been retired from the show ring for several years. Nevertheless, he was one of several dogs invited to go back to Philadelphia in October 1991, two days before the National Specialty, to take part in a video, produced by the American Kennel Club, featuring the Breed Standard of the West Highland White Terrier. The Bosos had got Nicky in good coat and condition, and so they decided to enter him in the Veteran Class at the National Specialty held at Montgomery County. It speaks volumes for their kennel management and the condition of their dog, that he not only won the Veteran Class but went on to be awarded Best of Breed, while being handled by his owner

Chapter Thirteen

WESTIES IN SCANDINAVIA

FINLAND

West Highland White Terriers have been in Finland since the thirties, but it is only fairly recently that the breed has really taken off. To say the breed is popular in this country is putting it rather mildly; I would be more inclined to say the Finnish people are fanatical about Westies. The size of the country as a land mass is quite large, but the total population in Finland is approximately that of the city of London – about five million people. When you take this into consideration, I think the membership of the Westie Club, which is some four hundred and still growing, is quite remarkable.

The first Westies were imported from England by Arne Louna's Kiho-Kennels in Tyrvaa; this was in exchange for Finnish Spitzes. The whole of the Louna Westie kennel was based on Kiho Topper and Sarumcote Denice, and, through inbreeding, the breed managed to establish itself and survive the war. The Louna line continued to increase after the war and were shown up to the fifties. The very first Westie to become a Champion was a bitch called Kiho Jeli, who gained her title in 1944. This was followed by a second Champion, bred by the same kennel, named Kiho Teddy Taapero, and owned by Liisa Vanhakartano who lived in a town called Lempaala.

This lady bred a couple of litters in her Taapero kennels, and then imported a pair of Westies from the UK – Ch. Patreena Of Patterscourt and Ch. Pardy Of Patterscourt. In 1957 Hilkka Aunio from Pori imported a bitch, Ch. Brancey Of Branston, from the Dennises. Brancey's daughter, Ch. Casey also had a litter but, unfortunately, nothing came of these and interest in the breed waned to the point where it nearly died out for a time in Finland.

In the sixties a bitch called Ch. Wolvey Proton was imported by Marita Palmu of Stigellhouse. This gave the breed a new start and created new interest. Proton had several litters and her name continued to appear in most of the Finnish pedigrees right up to the eighties. Jorma Sotavalta imported a dog, Int. and Nord. Ch. MacMahons White Trump from Sweden. This dog was shown very successfully in the early sixties, gaining many admirers along the way, some of whom began breeding Westies. At the end of the sixties the leading kennel was Margit Schroder of Whitecoat prefix. She imported several dogs from Britain including Ch. Famecheck Poltergeist, Whitebriar Jyrki, Int. and Nord. Ch. Alpinegay Ramona and Int. and Nord. Ch. Alpinegay Debonair. This lady was also successful in breeding a number of her own Champions. Other Westie breeders who started up at this time were: Ingrid Kalima of the Von Kibe kennel, Anja Kari of Mac Gillie and Jenny Paananen of Nera Bianca. Anja Kari began with imports from Sweden, but by the end of the decade she imported from Britain a winning stud dog, Int. and Nord. Ch. Alpinegay Galaxy. Ingrid Kalima also started with a bitch from Sweden, Ch. Grandawestis Gina. This was followed by Ch. Tweed Tomahawk and Tweed Temptation, who was a very important foundation bitch for the Von Kibe line. Jenny Paananen's first bitch was Wolvey Proton's daughter, Cindy. However, Jenny was soon to import some Westies from England – Ch. Strathairlie Silver Mark and a bitch, Ch. Lasara Lanima. The dog was very popular with a number of breeders. The bitch was of more significance to the Nera Bianca kennel itself.

The seventies saw the West Highland White Terrier really take off in Finland, with a record number of registrations being reached by the mid-seventies. There were a number of kennels which bred several litters a year; these were principally Von Kibe, Nera Bianca and Arjan, with the occasional litter being bred by the smaller breeders. The Mac Gillie kennel also continued to be active during this period. Imports at the beginning of the seventies by Nera Bianca included Int. and Nord. Ch. Alpinegay Quadrille and Int. and Nord. Ch. Tasman Temptation. Ch. Gaywyn Salena and Tasman Temptation were both responsible for producing many Champions. Anja Kari imported Int. and Nord. Ch. Parkendcot Moon Penny at about the same time as Ingrid Kalima brought in a dog of the Birkfell line, Gleneyre Sweet William. Sweet William was owned by Ulla Lonnqvist, and he became an

International and Nordic Champion, continuing his winning ways right through to the veteran stage. Anja Svensson brought Int. and Nord. Ch. Hardly Highland from Sweden, which was of particular importance to the Nera Bianca kennel. His best known descendant is Int. and Nord. Ch. Nera Bianca Butterfly. Eila and Erkki Myllyla (Arjan) in Oulu started with the bitch, Diana, but soon acquired more bitches from Mac Gillie and Von Kibe kennels. This was soon followed by the importation of a stud dog from England, Int. and Nord. Ch. Alpinegay Pizzicato; this dog can be called the ancestor of Finland's northern line of Westies. Arjan Lilian (by Alpinegay Galaxy) was the first Finnish-bred International Champion. In addition to the Arjan kennel, there was also another Westie kennel which featured in the northern territory, the Lumikiteen kennel, owned by Anneli and Timo Kettunen. Imports in the mid-seventies included Int. and Nord. Ch. Whitebriar Jevoranto to the Kettunens, and Nord. Ch. Whitebriar Johnsworthy to Jenny Paananen. Johnsworthy's best-known descendant is Int. and Nord. Ch. West-Air White Star. Von Kibe imported a dog, Ch. Birkfell Sergeant Pepper (owned by Gun Sjostrom), and Anja Svensson brought from Sweden Nord. Ch. Tweed Thistle Ranger who was sire to Nera Bianca Butterfly's dog puppy, Int. and Nord. Ch. Nera Bianca Bismarck. This was the most popular stud dog in Finland during the eighties. Nord. Ch. Maryglen Mountain Spirit and Ch. Maryglen Marigold were among Bismarck's descendants.

The eighties saw a sharp decline in the number of registrations of the breed in Finland. However, knowledge in showing and breeding Westies increased, and untrimmed Westies became a thing of the past and were no longer seen in the show ring. The Arjan kennels imported the dog Melwyn Fozzy Bear from the Birkfell kennel, and at the same time Ch. Arjan Super Star was having his influence on the Westies in the north of the country. The first Olac Westies arrived in Finland at the beginning of the eighties. Marianna Maki (Maryglen) in Lempaala imported a bitch, Ch. Olac Moonsong, and Jenny Paananen imported a dog from the same kennel, Nord. Ch. Olac Moonglen, which became one of the most popular stud dogs in the eighties. He was successfully used by many breeders, and the Olac Westies were of greatest influence in the Maryglen kennels, in particular. Some two years later, another top winning bitch was imported to this kennel, Nord. Ch. Olac Moonopal. A bitch, Ch. Maryglen Morning Glory (Moonglen – Moonopal), has very promising progeny in this kennel. The Maryglen kennels also have a long line of home-bred bitches, starting from Int. and Nord. Ch. Tasman Temptation's daughter, Ch. Nera Bianca Brenda's Charme. One of the show stars of the early eighties was Raimo Louhio's Swedish import, Int. and Nord. Ch. Times Fuzzy Magic. Sweden exported another highly influential dog into Finland around this time – Nord. Ch. Bushey's

Mister O'Tom. In the mid-eighties a number of bitches were imported. Amongst these was Leena Kulmala's Ch. Riwals Special Copy, who had a litter by Fuzzy Magic and produced Raija Jarvinen's line bitch (Raijaj), Ch. Hillman's Time To Thank. Nera Bianca imported Ch. Lasara Laydydah and the Lazydays kennel brought Int. Ch. Lucilette Of Lasara Lazydays and also imported two dogs from Sweden, Ch. Riwals Rockabilly and Ch. Smash Big Wig. The end of the eighties saw the Maryglen kennel importing another dog from the UK, Ch. Domaroy King's Ransom, who for the last couple of years has been the most popular stud dog in Finland and has already sired a number of Champions. Veli-Pekka Kumpumaki started with a bitch, Nord. Ch. Ingrids Iris von Kibe, and followed this up with the importation of an English dog, Ch. Wistmill White Cockade. This dog has made his mark by siring a dog which has gained his title, Ch. Perhaps Passing Mist. Another successful dog in this kennel is Ch. Perhaps Crimetime. Imports in the late eighties have also included Juha Smolander's Ch. Pajazzo Kate O'Mara from Sweden, and the dog Ch. Birkfell Snow-In-Summer, along with a bitch Ch. Birkfell Silver Sequin, both coming from Sheila Clelland in England. Juha Smolander's Kazbar kennel has not, as yet, produced many puppies. Markku Tiisijarvi (Westlake) first imported a bitch, Ch. Famecheck Northern Lights, and then a dog, Ch. Vogrie Glen Tara. Raili Kaikkonen (Riley's) imported Ch. Blossom Of Famecheck. Before the borders were closed between Finland and Sweden, due to a rabies outbreak, the Raijaj kennel tended to use Swedish stud dogs. This kennel's leading bitch is Ch. Raijaj You're Welcome, who is by Ch. Norwest Mr. Hurricane out of Time To Thank. One of the most popular stud dogs at the end of the eighties was Ch. Westlake Ettrickboy.

It was during the eighties that many of the old, larger kennels gradually faded out. The last Champion from Arjan was Ch. Arjan Herbert in 1988. Ingrid Kalima's last import from Britain, Ch. Famecheck Popstar, was used only a few times before she decided to live part of each year in Spain. She also took with her the last bitch, Int. Ch. Churriana, sired by Ch. Olac Moonglen. After dropping out of the dog scene for a while, Jenny Paananen has made a new start by importing a new bitch puppy from Scotland, Lymehill Sea Anemone. The new leading kennels of the eighties were Marianna Maki's Maryglen, Ulla and Leif Lonnqvist's Lazydays and perhaps Veli-Pekka Kumpumaki's. However, kennels are not producing large numbers of puppies, which can only be for the good of the breed. All Westie breeding is now done at a domestic level.

The beginning of the nineties has seen a lot of activity in the show scene. New dogs have been imported, such as Juha Smolander's Ch. Zino's Just Jimmy, Birgit Juura's Ashgate Shinnes, Paivi Iltanen's Ashgate Dippin and Ritva Ikonen's Ch. Handsome Indy. Marianna Maki also has a new bitch puppy, Domaroy High Flyer

(Ch. Olac Moonpilot – Domaroy Soraya). The Swedish exhibitors were frequent participants at Finnish shows up to the late eighties, but were then unable to continue because of the new rabies frontier. The Swedish Westies, always known as being of excellent quality and high in presentation, collected a large number of wins in Finland. Over the years, many Finnish bitches have been mated to Swedish dogs, but unfortunately the new restrictions make this impossible. Frontiers to the rest of Europe are now open, but to date, little use has been made of this new possibility. Registrations for Westies are now very buoyant, and the highest total for many years was recorded in 1991. The popularity of the Westie in Finland has meant that demand for puppies has always exceeded supply. Fortunately, the size of litters, which was very small in the eighties, is now rising, with an average of five per litter recorded in 1991.

NORWAY

In 1931 the first Norwegian-owned Westie was shown in Norway – an English import named Clin Citronate. Since that time a lot of Westies have been imported, most of them coming from Swedish and English kennels. In 1955 the first Famecheck dog arrived, and in 1976 Olac Moongem was imported followed by Whitebriar Jeanoake in 1979. It was these last two bitches which seemed to give a fresh start to the breed in Norway. In 1984 two dogs were imported: Eng. Ch. Rotella Mighty Mike and Olac Moon Falcon. Moon Falcon, who became an International and Nordic Champion, gained high acclaim with nineteen Best of Breeds, seven Best of Group, one Best in Show, and even winning a Best in Show as a veteran. Other Westies have since been imported from the Olac, Ashgate, Arnholm, Lasara, Windcliffe, and Famecheck kennels.

The Norwegian Westie Club is presently an unofficial club, founded by a number of dedicated people in 1979. In comparison with the other Scandinavian Westie clubs it is relatively small, but the members have tremendous enthusiasm for the breed. Their present membership stands at approximately 180, but interest is growing all the time, as can be seen by the total registrations with the Norwegian Kennel Club. In 1988 sixty-eight dogs were registered, with five of these being imported. This was followed in 1989 by one hundred and one registrations, including twenty-three imports. Registrations in 1990 stood at seventy, with six imports, giving a total of seventy-six. It is interesting to compare these figures with other Terrier registrations over the same period, and to discover that this equals thirteen per cent of all Terriers registered in 1988, fifteen per cent in 1989, and fourteen per cent in 1990. All the indications show the Westie is becoming a much more popular breed in Norway, not only for showing but also as a pet. It seems that quite a number of kennels who previously bred larger types of breeds, are changing over to smaller breeds, with the Westie proving to be one of the most popular.

Prominent in the Westie show world are a number of major kennels, who have consistently been in the list of Top Ten breeders over the last five years. They include: Wenrick's (Wenche and Heidi Hagen), Charmabo (Marianne and Borre Andersen), Oaklund (Sidsel and Thore Lovlie), Pot Luck's (Kari and Odd Aronsen), Black Horn's (Gerd and Jarl Anthonisen), and Mar-Kri (Randi and Einar Andreassen).

There are other Westie enthusiasts who are working hard with both their showing and breeding programmes. They include: Martas (Karin Berntsen), Havglott (Kleppe), White Hills (Doris Vik), Ingierodden (Liv and Andreas Westby), Pizzicato (Georg Schultz), Skotteline (Turid and Bjorn Thorkildsen), plus Reidunn Aril, Johan Marheim and Borre Anderson.

The top Westie currently being shown in Norway is Nor. Ch. Wenrick's Jazzman (Swed. Ch. Lasara Looks-A-Smash – Int. Nor. Ch. Wenrick's Incidental Music), belonging to Rolf and Arild Anda. Following closely on his heels is Marianne and Borre Andersen's Nor. Ch. Olac Moonwren (Eng. Ch. Olac Moonpilot – Eng. Ch. Olac Moon Poppy). Moonwren has been the top winning Westie bitch in Norway in 1988 and 1989. Other dogs making an impact on the show scene include: Charmabos White Symphony (Nor. Ch. Arnholm Added Attraction – Nor. Ch. Olac Moon Poppy), Nor. Ch. Cona Glen Of Ashgate (Ashgate Fin Me Oot – Princess In White), Ashgate Beacravick (Ashgate Connel – Ashgate Bran Bright Lass), and Nor. Ch. Olac Moonglow On Mar-Kri (Olac Moonmaverick – Olac Wintermoon).

SWEDEN

The West Highland White Terrier was first included in the Swedish Kennel Club Stud Book in 1913, but there were only a few isolated dogs. Serious breeding of the Westie did not start until around 1930, with a number of dogs being imported from the UK. These were obtained from well known kennels of the time, such as Clint, Brean and Wolvey. The real turning point for the breed came when the Scottish Terrier breeder, Mrs Barbro Eklund of the famous Mac Mahon kennel introduced Westies to her kennels. This lady was not only a very clever breeder of Scottish Terriers, but she was also highly skilled with her presentation and handling in the show ring. All this expertise was also then given to her Westies, and people began to take more notice of these small, well presented, snowy-white dogs. The result was

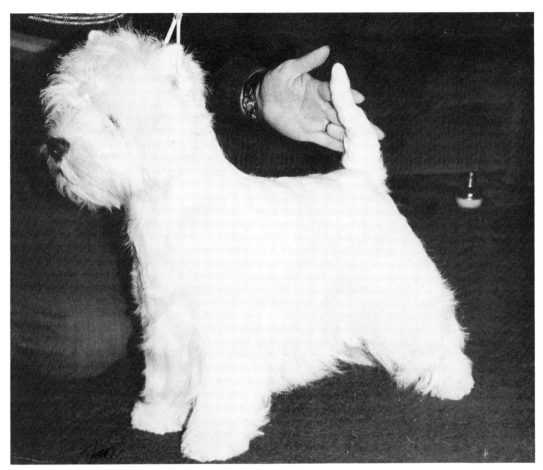

Eng. Int. Nord. Ch. Tweed Tartan Caledonia.

that the breed started to gain in popularity, with more people wanting to own and exhibit Westies. Unfortunately, not many puppies were being born, and Mrs Eklund would only sell her puppies to people she felt sure would show them, and then incorporate them into a well-researched breeding programme. One of the trusted few was Birgitta Hasselgren of the now famous Tweed kennel. She bought her first Westie from Mrs Eklund in 1962, and went on to show and breed from the bitch. At the time Birgitta was only a teenager, and she had to learn the hard way. However, I know that she is now very thankful for this early introduction into the dog scene. One of Birgitta's past Champions, who enjoyed a great show career, was Eng. Swed. Ch. Tweed Tartan Caledonia. He was possibly one of her top winning dogs, and I used him at stud when he was in England gaining his English Champion title. He has sired a lot of Champions in Sweden, and has also sired a number of Champions in England.

It was during the sixties and the seventies that the breed took off in Sweden, and, unfortunately, the result was that a lot of dog dealers started in the breed, and all for the wrong reasons. People were not prepared to wait a year for a Westie, so they bought any puppy, and at any price. This is never a good trend for any breed, but is very difficult to do anything about. Westies soon became the most popular terrier breed in Sweden, but Cairns have now taken over this dubious title. However, Westies are still ever-popular and a lot of new breeders are becoming involved with the breed all the time. The situation is currently made more difficult for breeders because of a ruling by the Swedish Westie Club which states that a stud dog can only be used on a limited number of bitches. Obviously, this means that the top stud dogs can no longer be used after they have had their quota of bitches, leaving the poorer quality dogs to be used instead. I believe fervently that the whole object of breeding and showing is to try and better the breed, and I fail to see how this can be achieved by using poorer quality stock. However, the majority of Swedish people are very dedicated to improving the breed, and they will not be content with second-best. Many Swedish pet owners show their dogs, to a much greater extent than in the UK, and this explains the lack of uniformity in type. Owner-exhibitors in the UK generally also tend to trim and prepare their own dogs, whereas many Swedish people take their dogs to a professional trimmer for a show trim. These professional trimmers also run courses on handling, so people attend the shows quite well prepared for the job in hand.

The Swedish Westie Club, Westie Alliansen, was founded in 1965, and to date it has over 1000 members with seven local clubs. The club is a very active organisation and rules the Westie fraternity with a firm hand, arranging many well attended breeders meetings. Each year the club holds its Championship show, and a British breed specialist is invariably invited to judge well-supported classes, with an overall entry in the region of one hundred dogs being the norm. The club is also very active in the distribution of information about Westies, and gives encouragement to newcomers by arranging many activities. They also produce a quarterly newsletter called *Westie Nytt*, which is a fifty-page booklet containing many photographs and much useful information. British breeders have exported a lot of good dogs over the years, and these have contributed to the quality of Swedish-bred dogs. It would be impossible to name them all, but the main influences over the later years have been: Lasara, Birkfell, Incheril, Melwyn, Famecheck, Ashgate, and more recently Domaroy and Tasman.

Of all the many fine dogs that have been produced over the years in Sweden, there is one which we must salute and give a special mention to. He is Int. Nord. Ch. Bushey's Magic Storm (Int. Nord. Ch. Birkfell Storm Song – Int. Nord. Ch. Melwyn

*Int. Nord. Ch.
Bushey's Magic
Storm with
Helene Hulthen.*

Muppet). This dog was bred by Britta Roos-Borjesson and went on to have a long and successful show career, culminating in winning top dog all-breeds in 1982. His last major wins were Best in Show three years running, 1987, 1988 and 1989 at the Skansen Show – the Swedish Terrier Club's most prestigious show. These wins were achieved from the veteran classes when he was seven, eight and nine years of age. He is the top winning Swedish-bred terrier of all time, and I share a little pride in this dog's achievements because he was the grandson of my first Champion, Ch. Olac Moonraker.

Other leading breeder-exhibitors in Sweden include Catherine Nilsson with her Times kennel. Catherine has been winning handsomely with her young bitch Swed. Ch. Times Super Trouper (Int. Nord. Ch. Times Lots of Magic – Ch. Times Press Image). She also co-owns Eng. Swed. Ch. Domaroy Suzerain with Mr and Mrs Roy Wilshaw. This dog won quite nicely in England before leaving for Sweden, where he has continued his winning ways. Lennart and Carin Nordlander of the Season kennel

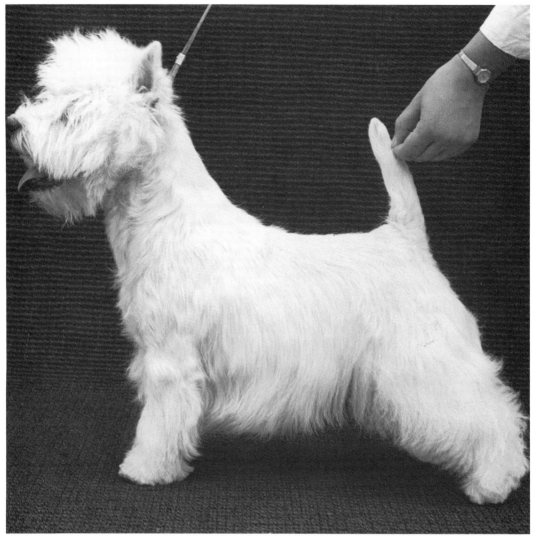

Int. Nord. Ch. Times Super Trouper.

bred Ch. Season Summer Opus (Yatzy Honky Tonk – Season Jessamine Summer Special), and he is now owned by Mrs H. Tegner-Apelberg. They also have Ch. Tasman Gratification (Chatterdale Connoisseur Of Tasman – Reservation Of Tasman) which quickly gained his title after being imported from the Bonuses in Scotland. The Pajazzo kennel, belonging to Mrs Elsie Hultgren, has been producing a nice type of Westie. One such bitch was Ch. Pajazzo Mona Lisa (Int. Nord. Ch. Season Join Tartan Summer – Harlekins Mammamia), who won Best in Show at the 25th Swedish Westie Club Championship Show in 1990 under our the British judge, Mrs Barbara Graham.

Tasman Acquisition.

Tasman Graduation.

Swed. Ch. Season Winter Unique (Tasman Acquisition – Tasman Graduation).

Louise Westerberg, with her Smash Kennel, has also enjoyed success in the last few years. Louise has always tried to produce quality dogs, and I am pleased to say her success rate has been first class. Recently, three dogs have stood out from this kennel. Firstly, Int. Nord. Ch. Smash I Am Sparking (Lasara Light Feet – Swed. Ch. Playing The Chorus Girl) who was Top Westie in 1990, and was Top Terrier in the same year. He travelled to Denmark to be exhibited at the National Terrier Show and won Best In Show. He has already sired Champions in Finland, Denmark and in his

Swed. Ch. Pajazzo Mona Lisa.

home country too. One of his sons, bred by Louise, is Swed. Ch. Smash Scally Wag, who is from a mating with Smash Hot Lips. This dog came to the fore in the show ring before his father, and was Westie of the Year in 1989, and third Top Terrier in the same year. The highlight of his show career was winning Best in Show at Gothenborg in 1989. The last of Louise's star trio is Swed. Ch. Smash Turbo (Swed. Ch. Smash Scally Wag – Lasara Lovers Choice). This dog completed a hat-trick for the kennel when he won the Westie of the Year in 1991 and was Best in Show at the

Int. Nord. Ch. Smash I Am Sparking.

Swed. Ch. Smash Scally Wag.

Swed. Ch. Smash Turbo.

Westie Club show in 1989 and 1990, and Best in Show at the Terrier Club show in Gothenborg. His winning tally includes seven Best of Breeds, three Groups and two Best in Show awards.

Joan and I have been very fortunate in having had a short stay in all three Scandinavian countries, and I can honestly say we have always been made most welcome and made to feel completely at home. The hospitality has been superb, and I only hope they have the same feelings when they visit England. Sweden has been very strong in the breed for many years now, with Finland gaining ground very rapidly in their expertise and quality of dogs. Norway, where their club membership is relatively small in numbers compared with enthusiasts in other countries, and especially with their neighbours, shows a great love and keenness for the breed. The breeders and exhibitors in all three countries deserve every success.

Chapter Fourteen

HEREDITARY FAULTS AND AILMENTS

Unfortunately, as in all breeds, there are hereditary faults in Westies. There is no point in trying to bury your head in the sand, pretending that this is not the case, and that everything in the garden is rosy. It is the responsibility of all Westie breeders to be honest, not only with themselves, but also with others, in a bid to eliminate these faults from the breed; and this can be achieved by a careful and selective breeding programme. After all, the welfare of the dogs should be a breeder's first concern, and producing strong, healthy pups should be the principal objective. It is widely recognised that when a breed becomes popular, there is a dramatic increase in congenital defects due, in the main, to indiscriminate breeding. Unfortunately, there are always unscrupulous people, whose overriding interest in breeding dogs is financial gain. The Westie is gaining in popularity by leaps and bounds, both in the UK and abroad, and we should all be vigilant and take extra care with the people we have dealings with. I have noticed that the bad press associated with large, guarding dogs, particularly in the UK, coupled with the extra costs of rearing large breeds, has resulted in a number of breeders switching to smaller breeds. I would not suggest, for one minute, that there is anything wrong with this, providing it is done for the right reasons. Frequently, people decide to change from one breed to another, for quite legitimate reasons. However, it is up to all of us, who have the welfare of the breed at heart, to ensure that all the stock we sell goes to responsible, caring owners.

LEGGE PERTHES DISEASE

This condition in dogs was first diagnosed by a Dutchman, and is generally referred to as Legge Perthes or just plain Perthes. It is a condition which can be found in young children as well as young dogs. The saddest and most unfortunate thing about this disease is the timing of its appearance in a puppy. You can have what appears to be a strong, healthy puppy one day, and the next day a puppy could be walking on only one of its hind legs. The leg which is obviously being carried will show definite signs of muscle wastage in the thigh. The condition usually strikes at any time from the age of four months up to twelve months of age. The cause of the problem is a starvation of blood supply to one of the hip joints, and a general deterioration or dying of the head of the femur bone. A wasting takes place, with the head of the femur trying to rotate in its unlubricated socket. There are differing schools of thought on whether this is an hereditary fault or not. I think it would be true to say that the majority of responsible breeders would withdraw a dog from stud if the condition was found in three different litters the dog had sired, to three different bitches of completely differing pedigrees. Similarly, a bitch which produced puppies with Perthes in three litters from three different stud dogs, should also be withdrawn from any future breeding programme. However, I am reliably informed by my veterinarian, that the veterinary universities do not consider this to be an hereditary disease. It has been suggested this condition could be caused through a knock, suffered by a young puppy while playing. If this is so, then I can readily accept that there is an hereditary weakness in the area which supplies blood to the affected joint. I believe the condition can be rectified to a degree by surgery. This entails the removal of the femur head, whereupon the femur starts growing spurs, or recalcification takes place, and within a short period of time, the puppy is able to walk again. In all the years we have been breeding, I have only ever seen one case of Perthes, and I would be quite happy never to see it again – the affected puppy seemed to be in quite a lot of pain.

CRANIOMANDIBULAR OSTEOPATHY (CMO)

This is quite a mouthful to say, and therefore the condition is generally referred to as CMO. There is a common misconception that this is a cancer of the jaw. It is, in fact, a calcification of the joint between the lower jaw and the skull. In layman's terms, this means that at this specified point, the jaw bone grows much larger than it should. This causes considerable pain to the puppy, and it also restricts the movement of opening the jaw and the process of chewing. The condition usually starts to occur in puppies when they are changing their teeth at approximately sixteen weeks of age, and onwards. It can occur in one side of the jaw, or both, and as you would expect with pain experienced in the jaw, it also affects the skull and ears. I have never seen a case of CMO, but I understand it can begin to abate after teething is completed. I believe this is considered to be an inherited disease, but there is no definite confirmation of this, so I would simply urge breeders to be vigilant, and to think twice before breeding from stock which they suspect has this condition in its line.

CLEFT PALATE

As with CMO, this is a condition I have never seen, so I can only pass on the description and information which has been given to me. This abnormality is found in new-born puppies, and the first sign is usually when milk runs back out of the puppy's nose when it is suckling from its mother. It is caused when the roof of the mouth fails to close, leaving an opening from the mouth into the nasal passage. It is extremely rare for a puppy to survive this complaint because they invariably die of starvation or from pneumonia. It has been suggested this condition is an hereditary abnormality, and once again I would advise breeders to be cautious with any stock that has produced the abnormality in previous litters.

COPPER TOXICOSIS

This would seem to be an hereditary, copper-associated liver disease, which has been associated with Bedlington Terriers for a number of years. It has been recognised in the United States since 1979 (Twedt and others 1979), and in the UK (Kelly and others 1984), and is now being found in certain bloodlines of West Highland White Terriers in the United States (Thornburg and others 1984). Affected animals develop hepatitis and eventually liver cirrhosis. The disease is due to an autosomal recessive gene (Johnson and others 1980) that results in faulty copper excretion from the liver (Le-Chu and others 1982).

In brief, the scientists examined necropsy tissue from five Westies which had died from cirrhosis of the liver. All five had an abnormally high hepatic copper concentration. They also examined liver biopsy tissue from sixty-six asymptomatic Westies, ranging in age from ten days to fourteen years. Normal dogs have hepatic copper concentration of less than 400 parts per million (ppm) on a dry weight basis. Copper concentrations ranged as high as 3500 ppm among the Westies. Two of the Westies which had died from cirrhosis were mother and daughter. Twenty-two of the dogs in their study were closely related to these two dead dogs. Matings between animals with high liver concentration resulted in pups that had high copper concentration. The copper-associated disease in Westies is inherited. A male Westie with hepatic copper concentration of 1750 ppm dry weight was mated to a normal Beagle bitch (hepatic copper concentration 360 ppm dry weight) and three pups were produced. At five and a half months old, the hepatic copper concentrations in the pups were 600, 700, and 930 ppm dry weight. These results indicate that hereditary copper toxicosis may be a dominant trait in Westies.

The results of this study were included in a letter sent to and published in *The Veterinary Record*, dated January 25th, 1986, written by Dr L. P. Thornburg and Mrs S. J. Crawford, both of the University of Missouri, USA. The purpose of the letter was to alert veterinarians in the UK to the existence of this hereditary copper-associated disease in Westies. They state that some of the affected dogs in their study were obtained from kennels in the UK.

UMBILICAL HERNIA

The very first Westie I bought had an umbilical hernia. I was an absolute novice at the time, and I did nothing about it. I had no ambitions to either breed from her or show her, so the question of an operation never arose, especially as she never showed signs of any discomfort. An umbilical hernia can best be described as a fairly soft swelling near the navel, where part of the stomach is protruding through the stomach wall, which has failed to close after birth. It is possible for this opening to close up as the puppy grows older, or if a small hole remains open, it can be small enough for it to cause no trouble. Obviously, if it is a large hernia, you should seek professional advice from a vet.

INGUINAL HERNIA

This type of hernia will be found as a swelling in the groin, and in either side of the dog. The inguinal hernia is more serious than the umbilical hernia, and should, at all costs, be checked by a vet. This type of hernia is more common in older dogs, but unfortunately, if it is found in a small puppy, it is usually necessary to remove one of the testicles during surgery in order to correct the problem.

KERATO CONJUNCTIVITIS SICCA (DRY EYE)

This condition has become apparent in Westies over the past ten years, according to Dr Stephen D. Carrington, who is carrying out research into the problem. The disease starts in animals aged between two and seven years old as a recurrent form of conjunctivitis, and people who have witnessed this condition say it is chronic, and very painful.

In 1986 Dr Carrington came along to a Westie club show, and he stayed all day carrying out tests to detect this condition on a large number of dogs, with the owners' consent. Obviously, it was very pleasing for all concerned that the tests proved negative, but it is a condition we are all going to have to watch out for and try to eliminate from the breed. In his report, written after the series of tests he carried out at the Westie show, Dr Carrington states that the condition is probably due to an abnormality of the immune system, which becomes directed against the glandular tissues which secrete the middle watery layer of the tear film. As the level of tear secretion gradually falls, the pre-corneal tear film becomes unstable, the cornea becomes hazy due to inflammation, and a copious sticky mucous discharge is seen. With further reductions of tear secretion, which may be cyclical, blood vessels and pigment grow over the cornea and the dog slowly loses its sight.

Treatment for the condition is initially by drugs, which increase secretion of tears by supplementing artificial tear solutions. However, eventually the level of tears falls so low that treatment of this nature becomes impractical. Surgical treatment is possible, but it involves transplanting the duct of the parotid salivary gland from the mouth to the eye, thus causing the dog to have 'salivary tears'. Obviously, this is a very distressing disease, and as breeders of Westies we should do all we can to eliminate it from the breed.

MONORCHIDISM OR CRYPTORCHIDISM

These terms are used with reference to male dogs which have either one testicle, or both testicles, not fully descended into the scrotum. Ideally, both testicles should be descended into the scrotum at birth, but it is not uncommon for a male puppy to have his testicles tucked high up in the groin. It is then that you may encounter trouble, if one, or even both testes, fail to drop down. The main causes for this are:

1. The spermatic cord gets tied into a knot during formation, preventing the testis from dropping into place.
2. The spermatic cord is not long enough to allow full descent into the scrotum.

3. If a puppy has an inguinal hernia, this could also be the reason for the testis not descending, as it is blocked on its journey down. When a puppy is operated on for this type of hernia, it usually necessitates the removal of this testicle.

It is highly recommended by the veterinary profession that a testis or testes which have not dropped into position should be removed by surgery, as they can become cancerous. There are differing schools of thought on whether monorchidism or cryptorchidism in dogs is hereditary. In humans it is a birth defect. The English Kennel Club deem it an hereditary fault, and until quite recently it would not allow a monorchid dog or a dog which had been castrated to be shown. However, all that has now been changed and both types are considered eligible to enter for competition. As I have already stated, the whole object of breeding and showing dogs is supposedly for the improvement and betterment of the breed; consequently the Kennel Club's reasoning on this completely escapes me.

MANGE

There are a number of ideas circulating as to the cause or causes of this complaint, but I think it is fair to say it is an allergy, and it can be either parasitic or non-parasitic in origin. Once we accept this, then we must also accept that the causes are limitless. As with humans there can be so many reasons for allergenic skin problems. The allergy can be caused by any number of things in the home, for instance, household plants, the stuffing used in cushions, nylon carpets, curtain material, a warm, dry atmosphere due to central heating; sometimes the dog's blood can be over-heated, which leads to an allergic reaction, and even the diet you feed could be a factor. However, let us start with one of the most obvious causes, which is fleas or other parasites. These are simple to diagnose and to treat. Explain the problem to your vet, and you will be given a suitable medicated shampoo. There are also sprays available, which can be very effective in killing off parasites. One of the major problems is mites, which burrow under the skin, living and breeding there, with the complete cycle taking just a few days. Quite often you will see a dog with inflamed areas of skin around the inside of the rear legs, and under the armpits of the front legs. The dog will also be doing a lot of scratching in these areas. This is Sarcoptic mange and should be treated by the vet. The most vulnerable dogs to this condition are those that are generally run down or in poor health.

One complaint common to many Westies is the ear mange, Otodectic, and it is a bane to most owners. It is an extreme irritant, causing the dog to scratch incessantly. If it is left untreated for any length of time, the ear will become highly inflamed and swelling takes place, leading to the eventual closure of the ear. Providing you have not left it too long before treatment, the condition is easily treated by using ear drops which you can get from your vet. These drops loosen the wax and, with care, you will be able to clean out the ear with cotton-wool buds on sticks (cotton swabs). Unfortunately, if the condition is left untreated and the ear closes, then surgery may be necessary. I always have a bottle of ear drops in the medicine cupboard, and every now and again, I put a few drops down my dogs' ears to give them a good clean out.

Demodex Canis is probably one of the most difficult types of mange to cure. It appears most commonly in puppies when they are at the stressful stage of cutting their second teeth. It can also occur when a pup has or has had an illness, a time when it will be a little run down. The signs are first noticed as small balding patches on the head, e.g. round the eyes and on the skull. It will be necessary to improve the dog's general health, and to remove the hair from around the infected areas, and the burning of this hair is imperative. Demodex Canis can only be treated by a vet; it is very contagious and, therefore, a dog with this complaint must be isolated. It goes without saying that general hygiene is an absolute must at this point, which includes wearing different clothing whenever dealing with an infected dog, and making sure that you wash your hands thoroughly.

ACUTE OTITIS EXTERNA

If you see a Westie coming towards you, carrying its head and one of its ears on one side, then you can be pretty sure the problem is being caused by a foreign body in the ear – a grass seed or ear mites are the most common culprits. Please seek professional help as soon as possible. I live in the country, with nice, big fields at the rear of the house, and as soon as the farmer starts cutting the hay in the summer, one bitch, in particular, is highly susceptible to becoming infested with grass mites. These make her scratch so much that she gets inflamed areas over her body and loses her hair. Eventually, a solution was found in the form of a spirit-based lotion, applied to the affected areas, which kills the mites and soothes the inflammation. I have also found a product, which is specifically manufactured to deal with this problem, and I have found it to be excellent for completing the cure and for promoting the growth of new hair.

ANAL GLANDS

Occasionally, you may see a dog dragging its bottom along the ground; this is usually a sure sign that the dog is suffering from a problem with its anal glands. The anal gland becomes blocked and will need emptying. Get a large swab of cotton wool (cotton) and cover the anus with it. Put your thumb and first finger at approximately twenty minutes to four either side of the anus, and squeeze. This should clear the contents of the anal gland, but do be prepared for quite a stench. The general cause of this complaint is insufficient roughage in the diet.